Honor your father and your mother, so
the Lord your God is giving you.

EXODUS 20:12 (NIV)

There are those who curse their fathers
and do not bless their mothers;
those who are pure in their own eyes
and yet are not cleansed of their filth;
those whose eyes are ever so haughty,
whose glances are so disdainful;
those whose teeth are swords
and whose jaws are set with knives
to devour the poor from the earth,
the needy from among humankind.

PROVERBS 30:11-14 (NIV)

Stand up in the presence of the aged,
show respect for the elderly and revere your God.
I am the Lord.
When foreigners reside among you in your land,
do not mistreat them.
The foreigners residing among you
must be treated as your native-born.
Love them as yourself,
for you were foreigners in Egypt.
I am the Lord your God.
Do not use dishonest standards
when measuring length, weight or quantity.
Use honest scales and honest weights,
an honest ephah and an honest hin.
I am the Lord your God, who brought you out of Egypt.

LEVITICUS 19:32-36 (TNIV)

THE ECONOMICS OF HONOR

Biblical Reflections on Money and Property

Roelf Haan

Translated by

Bert Hielema

WILLIAM B. EERDMANS PUBLISHING COMPANY
GRAND RAPIDS, MICHIGAN / CAMBRIDGE, U.K.

Originally published as *Economie van de eerbied. Kanttekeningen bij het bijbelse spreken over geld en goed* (Delft: Meinema, 1985; enlarged edition, Zoetermeer: Meinema, 2005). Previously published in English as *The Economics of Honour* (Geneva: World Council of Churches, 1988, 1991).

This revised and enlarged edition of the English translation published 2009 by Wm. B. Eerdmans Publishing Co.
2140 Oak Industrial Drive N.E., Grand Rapids, Michigan 49505 /
P.O. Box 163, Cambridge CB3 9PU U.K.
www.eerdmans.com

Printed in the United States of America

15 14 13 12 11 10 09   7 6 5 4 3 2 1

Library of Congress Cataloging-in-Publication Data

Haan, Roelf L.
[Economie van de eerbied. English]
The economics of honor: biblical reflections on money and property /
Roelf Haan; translated by Bert Hielema.
p.   cm.
Includes bibliographical references and index.
ISBN 978-0-8028-6012-5 (pbk.: alk. paper)
1. Economics in the Bible.   I. Title.

BS670.H2313   2009
220.8′33 — dc22

2008043908

To my wife
Marijke de Haan

Contents

Contents

Introduction

B ible stories and biblical expressions are viewed in this book within the context of contemporary thinking. Current formulations of economic problems are placed next to biblical statements regarding security and technique, commerce and development, productivity and distribution, wealth and poverty. However, these annotations are not meant to contrast the contemporary situation with "the economy in the biblical era." The biblical message goes beyond happenings then and now; just as then, today, too, life is a faith journey and calls for fundamental choices. The focus in this book is on the spiritual meaning of our economic life. Its aim is to broaden insight into our modern society and focus on the place of the Christian community.

The book has four sections. The first introduces the biblical understanding of costs. The second considers the origin and nature of economic injustice in our world, recognizing that mere analysis of contemporary structures of "development" and oppression may lead to fanaticism, cynicism, or paralysis and passivity. The Bible does reveal these structures, but goes further, as I hope also to do. The third part of the book opens with a meditation on the fifth commandment, the command to honor your father and your mother. It is from this meditation that the book as a whole draws its title, *The Economics of Honor*. The fourth section elaborates more fully on today's economic world; it also includes two chapters on Jesus' parables, those of the talents and the pounds. Both these parables are often applied to current thinking about money by assimilating them to today's ruling "money motive," thus, I contend, robbing them of their real meaning.

I recommend that the reader keep a Bible handy, as I will refer frequently to numerous biblical passages. For the reader's convenience, an index of texts is part of this volume. Although the book forms an entity, each chapter has been written to stand on its own, and particular chapters or the whole book may be used for personal or group study. They may also serve as the basis for sermons; in fact, that is how this book was originally conceived. Emmanuel Levinas has said, "A sermon is not only a piece of literature, but also an essential form of human thinking."

The Brazilian author Rubem Alves once remarked, "I find the proposition obscene that we must fight for justice and food because theology has concluded this from holy writ. Those who fight for the poor because God says so, do not love the poor." He hits the nail on the head. Justice does not depend on being covered with Christian icing. The Bible is not a book that moralizes with a "must-do" attitude, but a book of faith. For this reason I have added an epilogue by an untainted witness.

It is my wish that the following pages may be read not only by those who are familiar with the Bible, but also by those who are not acquainted with this historic book that remains remarkably current. It is my additional wish that it may contribute to the discussion and implementation of a just economy, a sound societal structure, and the repair of human rights.

ROELF HAAN

PART I

The Risk of the Other

CHAPTER 1

Contemplating Cost

*Towards the beginning of harvest three of the thirty chiefs went down
to join David at the cave of Adullam, while a band of Philistines was
encamped in the valley of Rephaim. David was then in the stronghold; and the garrison of the Philistines was then at Bethlehem. David said longingly, "O that someone would give me water to drink
from the well of Bethlehem that is by the gate!" Then the three warriors broke through the camp of the Philistines, drew water from the
well of Bethlehem that was by the gate, and brought it to David. But
he would not drink of it; he poured it out to the LORD, for he said,
"The LORD forbid that I should do this. Can I drink the blood of the
men who went at the risk of their lives?" Therefore he would not drink
it. The three warriors did these things.*

2 SAMUEL 23:13-17

Around the end of the 1940s, Dr. J. Ridder, the general treasurer of the
Dutch Finance Ministry and a well-known Christian economist, was
asked to explain the essence of economics in a few words. As his point of
departure he chose the above passage from 2 Samuel, considering it a striking example of what Paul meant when he said, "Whether you eat or drink,
or whatever you do, do all to the glory of God" (1 Cor. 10:31).

I agree. There is hardly a better way to illustrate the core of economics
than by this story, in which the biblical vision so sharply deviates from any
other.

3

David's desire for a drink of water seems out of place among the battle tales that surround it, and this difference makes it intriguing. It's as if it has been added as a counterpoint, a contrasting argument, to distinguish it from the main element, included to break the monotony of recording the heroics of David and his top military men. The narrative concludes with the sentence, "The three warriors did these things," but the striking thing is not so much what these valiant men managed; rather, it is precisely David's unusual reaction that the author of this passage wants to convey to us.

Modern economics would have us believe that to act economically is a matter of rational analysis, of common sense. Economics, according to this view, is merely a matter of efficiency, nothing else but cutting cost to the bone. Lean and mean. It is automatically assumed that sound judgment and economic intuition point only one way: to our very own Western model as it has taken shape in contemporary history. No thought is given to any other possibilities. The idea that different cultures may prefer an alternative economic model is never entertained. The possibility of a Christian critique of the current economic orthodoxy is simply written off as unscientific, and thus irrational.

Our economic textbooks concern themselves with the rationality of consumer behavior. Their line of thinking goes a bit like this: when the consumer acts as a buyer, a sale takes place. This necessitates prior production and investment. The consumer, therefore, is sovereign: he or she rules the market and controls the production process. Of course, it is presupposed that the all-powerful consumer acts rationally as a "price-conscious" being, wanting to get the most for his or her money. Thus our educational system and the entire commercial advertising machine are centered on the notion that the only way to be price-conscious is one of self-interest. All other ways are stupid, unscientific, and old-fashioned.

One economist relates the story of a medieval monk, who, as a child of his time, did not possess this sort of economic price-consciousness.

He had been on a pilgrimage to Rome and, while traveling, had bought a silver chalice, intending to place it in his hometown cathedral. On his way home to Germany he showed his purchase to two merchants who were traveling with him, and mentioned to them what he had paid for his treasure. The market-wise traders congratulated him on his buy, calling it a real bargain, as he had gotten it for well below its real value. They were quite amused that this simple monk had unintentionally gotten a far better deal than they ever had. Yet when the monk heard the true worth of the chalice he was flabbergasted. He immediately left the traders and returned to Rome to pay the seller the difference. To him, being price-conscious meant paying the just price, the proper amount.[1]

The book in which this anecdote originally appeared wanted to illustrate the "irrational" influence religion can have on the economic act, and to make the argument that the two should never be intertwined. After all, economic theory has matured in modern times, and is perfectly capable to determine its own soundness of mind.

However, biblical thinking fundamentally clashes with every pretense of human rational "autonomy." Bible believers confess an all-seeing God. David's action would, by all accounts, be irrational if it were separated from his relationship with God. Unless we, together with David, confess the existence of a transcendental God, a God who is both above the world and who maintains a relationship with us humans, then, indeed, David pouring out this water appears a grotesque gesture.

So what really happens here, in this strange story? We see David act as consumer. He has what we call an "economic need." Simply put, he is thirsty, and, knowing the region where he grew up, recalls that he is close to the water well in his hometown of Bethlehem.

It could be that there was no other water source nearby. Perhaps he attached great sentimental value to this place — we do not know. Regardless, economic theory points to an economic need. David desires, and he cannot satisfy his craving by making a quick trip to the supermarket or the nearest Starbucks. Further, as commander-in-chief of his country's army he cannot leave his men and just do what he likes. The most logical course of action, therefore, would be to send out a few of his officers — all of whom would be eager to earn some brownie points — to fetch his drink, even though it is situated in enemy-occupied territory. In fact, he doesn't even give an order. Spontaneously three valiant men volunteer to fetch him the water he yearns for.

We need to remember, however, that there is no doubt what David wanted, and that he also would have known that, as king, his wish was effectively a command. He also would have known that his men were ready to risk their lives for him. He therefore remains responsible for the fate of the three heroes, in spite of their volunteering for this mission (in the

---

1. See Daniel R. Fusfeld, *The Age of the Economist* (Glenview, Ill.: Scott, Foresman, 1966).

same way as our market economy recognizes that labor commits itself "freely").

No doubt David's initial reaction was that he was in for a bargain. After all, the expedition would hardly cost him anything personally. Perhaps the three soldiers might have to postpone another assignment for the time being (economists call this the "opportunity cost"); perhaps they would be placing themselves in danger. Nevertheless, in view of his need and the available means, the entire enterprise would certainly be deemed rational.

The real surprise is what David does when he receives the water. After the heroes break through the enemy lines, successfully scoop up the water, and bring the result of their dangerous mission to David — in other words, after the daring raid succeeds — suddenly all logic goes out the window. David makes his men look like fools. All their bravery comes to naught; all their efforts have been fruitless.

"But David wouldn't drink it"! How come? David has suddenly become aware of something he hadn't thought of before. That is the crazy, yet liberating, part of this story. Only after his men are well on their way does he realize the true consequences of his request. And so, conscious of the tremendous risks involved, he effectively cancels it. David comes to his senses and realizes that he has ordered a good whose price is far too high: the cost to acquire it could be the very lives of the producers. He realizes that he has only paid attention to the price he himself would have to pay, without taking into account the possible cost to others. He had fully calculated his own risk, but not that of the laborer, the actual producer.

In this moment of reflection David has only one option: to turn to the Lord. It's not enough to offer apologies to the men whose lives he had endangered simply in order to satisfy a personal need, even though he is not obligated to do so in view of the hierarchical relationship he has with his subordinates. Indeed, more than likely this is a factor that even more frustrates the executors of this honorable mission: even though the plan had succeeded beyond expectation, it's all for nothing. He simply dumps the water. That precious water!

"The Lord forbid that I'll drink this. This isn't mere water, it's their lifeblood — they risked their very lives to bring it!" we can imagine David thinking. David realizes that his attitude before the face of the Lord was so irresponsible that he steps out of the production process and away from the consumption treadmill and abandons the societal position of power that had imprisoned him. Had he drunk this water, he would have ingested the blood of these men.

But wait — isn't that an exaggeration and too emotional? After all, no real blood was shed. Thank God: all had gone well. But David knows that God doesn't accept this sort of thanksgiving. So, showing that he is sorry and pledging that he will never repeat such an action, he pours out the water before the Lord, thanking him that not only the producers' lives have been spared, but that also he, as consumer, has seen the error of his ways. He, the consumer, is prepared to relinquish his consumption because the costs are unacceptable in the eyes of the Lord. In respect for their life he pours out the water, which could have meant the blood of the men (see the parallel in Deut. 12:24). Being sorry is always inefficient. It's much easier not to even try. But if you do? Then, by the grace of God, the inefficient path of being sorry leads to freedom. That's the path David follows.

What is at stake here is the biblical reasoning of cost calculation, of how to evaluate a bargain. My cost to buy a product is not the only one; there is more to it than that. According to current economic rationale, consumption can go on as long as the consumer is willing to pay the price that he or she has been charged. But that is simply an individualistic cost calculation, based on the belief that every consumer is sovereign, a person with her own authority to act as she likes. It is not necessarily rational, but it certainly is egoistic, self-absorbed, and centered on a manifestation of economic or political power.

For a Christian, contemplating the cost must be done *coram Deo*, before the face of God, with God looking over our shoulder. Only then do we see the real components that enter into the cost calculation: the environmental costs, labor conditions, risks to fellow humans, as well as the damage done to our own religious integrity.

This method of cost calculation is no less "rational" than that of material self-interest. Both involve economic evaluation and contemplation. The main difference lies in contemplating the true, all-around costs — that is, not merely individual interest and the personal purchasing power, but especially labor circumstances, working conditions, and environmental consequences under which the product has been manufactured.

Consuming rationally cannot be confined solely to being price-conscious, reasoning that if the price is too high, I will choose not to purchase. Consuming rationally means being aware of the cost. When those costs imperil the welfare of somebody else or of nature, then I must refrain from consumption. Is such an approach possible? Are there still "unspoiled" products, whether banking services, golden rings, or produce?

But that isn't the question. After all, the current economic model and rationale were not the only possibilities. "From the beginning" (Matt. 19:8) things were different, and therefore the conclusion is different also.

Our economic act must be directed towards instituting an economic framework geared toward the respect of the life and welfare of "the other." We require a model in which I, as consumer, as a neighbor to the person with whom I engage in an economic relationship, need not lose my integrity before the eye of the Creator.

As a start we should pour out before the Lord our existing economic accomplishments, acquired at minimal cost, as the life of human beings comes cheap. Do we really understand what these three heroes have done?

PART II

Economic Development

CHAPTER 2

Economic History

The word of the LORD *came to me: "Son of man, take up a lament concerning the king of Tyre and say to him: 'This is what the Sovereign* LORD *says: You were the model of perfection, full of wisdom and perfect in beauty. You were in Eden, the garden of God; every precious stone adorned you: ruby, topaz and emerald, chrysolite, onyx and jasper, sapphire, turquoise and beryl. Your settings and mountings were made of gold; on the day you were created they were prepared. You were anointed as a guardian cherub, for so I ordained you. You were on the holy mount of God; you walked among the fiery stones. You were blameless in your ways from the day you were created till wickedness was found in you. Through your widespread trade you were filled with violence, and you sinned. So I drove you in disgrace from the mount of God, and I expelled you, O guardian cherub, from among the fiery stones. Your heart became proud on account of your beauty, and you corrupted your wisdom because of your splendor. So I threw you to the earth; I made a spectacle of you before kings. By your many sins and dishonest trade you have desecrated your sanctuaries. So I made a fire come out from you, and it consumed you, and I reduced you to ashes on the ground in the sight of all who were watching.'"*

EZEKIEL 28:11-18 (NIV)

In the last chapter we saw that the best way to analyze the problem of economics from a biblical perspective was to start with the relationship between God and human beings. In this chapter I want to explore a dangerous, if common, misinterpretation of this understanding throughout the history of economics.

When our current prevailing economic thought was first being developed during the so-called Age of Enlightenment, theology had not much to do anymore with biblical faith. It believed in providence and in the hereafter. Belief in God was simply assumed. However, it was a belief that breathed the spirit of the Deism of that day. "Great and Eternal Supreme" — so begins Psalm 38 in one eighteenth-century translation. God no longer operated on a personal basis. He had been removed to a safe distance as Supreme, after assembling the world as a watchmaker does a watch. "No longer does the Creator look after his creation: the world has a momentum of its own, ruled by the laws of nature" — so went the prevailing wisdom.

That belief also maintained that Christendom was as old as creation: "In essence," as one historian writes, "it was nothing but a rational faith in God, in virtue and in immortality. The rest was invented by theologians and priests, and that mixture spoils the broth."

Adam Smith, the eighteenth-century economist who was the founder of modern economic science, and also a professor in natural theology, viewed God as just such a watchmaker, who had manufactured his creation and then put it on the market, so to speak, as a finished product. Such a man-made philosophy of creation, adapted to human image and likeness, is still proclaimed today, everywhere people prefer not be involved with an active and watchful God, a God always ready for dialogue. Those who hold this view may honor this Supreme Being as the shaping force of creation, but they don't want to honor him as the "Wonderful Counselor, Mighty God, Everlasting Father, Prince of Peace" of Isaiah 9:5, who continuously participates in his work of art. They forget that God on the seventh day not only rested, but also on that same day, the day in which we now live, is completing creation.

Contrary to Adam Smith–style reasoning, God stays in touch through his creative Word. For now the ball is in our court. We now are the managers, the responsible persons, the key people in the economy. That's how Israel saw it. Unlike the rulers of our earth, who used to have their statues erected as signs of their own divine authority, Israel saw *everyone* as having full divine powers, as being "made in his image and likeness." God created heaven and earth by his Word. And he maintains them by that same Word. Gerhard von Rad writes in his *Old Testament Theology*, "The only continuing connection between God and His creation work is the Word."[1]

However, the world has always wanted to see this differently. A good example of a creation philosophy devised by humans can be found in the official propaganda of the military dictatorship in Argentina, which started with the coup in 1976. The immediate result of this violent takeover was the collapse of the national economy. Until that time, Argentina had enjoyed a high level of widespread prosperity, thanks at least in part to a well-functioning labor movement. Yet within a few years of taking over, the junta caused this society to degenerate into near-total chaos. Not only were all human rights abolished, but also the entire national culture suffered through a reign of terror instigated by these cruel rulers. All of this was done in the name of national security: the generals viewed their every action as justified because they were blinded by their particular creation philosophy. In their warped minds they only saw that "in the beginning there was left-wing terrorism." At that point their thinking stopped — in the beginning!

Obsessed by the doctrine of national security, they single-mindedly believed that only armed intervention could transform prehistoric chaos into law and order. Their military mentality convinced them that they possessed a perfect mandate to extend their absolute power to all areas of life. This is typified by the stories of two women, as related in an English television broadcast, who escaped from one of hundreds of concentration camps the junta set up: the women said that their torturers continuously proclaimed, "Here we are God and we are the Law." This is a striking example of the demonic consequences for society when the creation revelation is distorted. Here we see how human beings, in an effort to secure their own place, justify their action by saying that their deeds are justified by absolute sovereignty, as if all men and women were not created in the image of God.

The modern economy has its own creation theology, as we can see from considering Adam Smith, one of its most important spokesmen. Smith saw human beings as "exchange animals." From the beginning, the most important human characteristic is the desire to trade, that is to say, to

---

1. Gerhard von Rad, *Old Testament Theology*, trans. D. M. G. Stalker (Edinburgh: Oliver & Boyd, 1962).

act in the market place. It is therefore in the market where we see genuine natural laws at work; we may not intermingle these laws with other ones, such as those of religion.

On this line of thinking, "nature" can tell us as much if not more than the Bible can about God. However, only those with a specialized education can understand these natural laws; common sense alone is not enough. What this really means is that an advanced degree in economics is required to be able to discuss economic problems. And this, of course, automatically disqualifies the church and her representatives, who are equipped only to deal with the supernatural, with the Supreme Being, with the immortal soul, with virtue.

This is not to say that the Deists and their successors had no need for religion. They needed it, but for a different purpose. Take Napoleon. Having risen to power, he began to exploit many of the church's teachings regarding servility and obedience for his own purposes. Likewise the generals in Latin America, whose life and thought already had been completely secularized, followed the same tactics once their coup had succeeded. They immediately stressed their faithfulness to the church, where they ostentatiously sat in the front pew whenever Mass was said on national holidays and television cameras were focused on them.

Our economic system today has a similar relationship with the church. It expects the ecclesiastical establishment to take a hands-off approach to economics, much as it assumes God takes a hands-off approach to the world. It believes that religion and economics are two separate fields with no common ground. Business is none of the church's business, as the church has no real understanding of what goes on in the world outside its doors.

It is for exactly this reason that the creation faith of the Old Testament clashes with the Western ideology of liberalism. Israel didn't believe that "heaven and earth" — that is, created reality — is a preprogrammed, harmonious order. Von Rad writes, "The world and what it contains finds its unity and internal cohesion not in the primary principle of cosmological order, but in Yahweh's absolute personal creative will."[2] By contrast, our economic textbooks maintain that the basis of economic life lies in the order of the "free market," which in turn obeys the eternal laws of nature, which, in turn, are grounded in human reason. Economic crises,

2. Von Rad, *Old Testament Theology*.

therefore, can be blamed on human failure to follow sufficiently this natural god.

However, the biblical creation story plainly shows that chaos and harmony, crisis and equilibrium, are all products of human history. Already in Eden God placed a decision before the man and the woman: either they could act according to his Word, or they could do differently. Crises are therefore not a product of laws of nature, simply embedded in God's creation. Rather, unemployment, poverty, pollution, mind-killing labor, and other negative byproducts of our economic order are not inevitable, occurring even in the best of all possible worlds, to be written off as unavoidable fate for the whole human race. They are instead the products of human history and human choices. Underdevelopment likewise cannot be blamed on the single factor of the malfunctioning of the market mechanism in some nations. That may be the current theory, but the reality is that it can be directly traced to centuries of colonial history.

As Christians, we owe our sense of history to our recognition of the significance of the Old Testament, which begins with the creation story. In the words of von Rad, "Israel fully recognized that she was being addressed by that sole divine power, and understood her origin to be His historical act. The long history of her various ups and downs is testimony that she saw herself a participant in the walk and talk with God, from the moment He started His dialogue with His people when leading her out of Egypt."[3]

Yet the accounts in Genesis 1 and 2 are not the only creation stories to be found in the Bible. We can find another one in Ezekiel 28, and it offers a clear indication that injustice does not originate with God. It so beautifully says, "You were the seal of perfection, full of wisdom and perfect in beauty. You were in Eden, the garden of God. . . . Your settings and mountings were made of gold; on the day you were created they were prepared." Here is an economy without a crisis, readymade for the human race. It was humanity that entered into sin, a sin which, as Ezekiel shows, becomes evident in widespread business dealings which have so often throughout history been associated with violence.

Indeed, rather than translate Ezekiel 28:18 to read "by your corrupt ways of doing business," as some understand it, the better way is to read "by the injustice of your trade," or "by your dishonest trade." Third World theologians have demonstrated how matters of interpretation such as this

---

3. Von Rad, *Old Testament Theology.*

can make the Bible appear to favor Western patterns of thinking, when in fact such is not the case.

We can't blame God and his creation. It was not so from the beginning. The fault lies with us, with human beings. The creation is not chaotic, even though today chaos is a constant threat. Belief in Genesis 1 and 2 places a choice before us: either live by the Word, that is, the creative and redemptive Word which originates with the same Creator and Sustainer. Or live by the current liberal ideology, which has fashioned its own creation concept and its own sense of history, which completely refutes the biblical idea of creation and history.

CHAPTER 3

The Economic Problem

Now Cain said to his brother Abel, "Let's go out to the field." And while they were in the field, Cain attacked his brother Abel and killed him.

Then the LORD said to Cain, "Where is your brother Abel?"

"I don't know," he replied. "Am I my brother's keeper?"

The LORD said, "What have you done? Listen! Your brother's blood cries out to me from the ground."

GENESIS 4:8-10 (NIV)

This is the message you heard from the beginning: We should love one another. Do not be like Cain, who belonged to the evil one and murdered his brother. And why did he murder him? Because his own actions were evil and his brother's were righteous. . . .

If anyone has material possessions and sees his brother or sister in need but has no pity on him or her, how can the love of God be in him?

1 JOHN 3:11-12, 17 (NIV)

These passages from Genesis and 1 John confront us immediately with the economic problem. It's the story of what we often call "the first sin": the first crime, the first murder. Death enters into the Bible as homicide, of which the victim is Abel, whose name means "breath of life."

Actually, sin came earlier. We read about it in the previous chapter, Genesis 3, to which some Bible translations assign the title "The First Sin." In most Bibles, the title for Genesis 4 simply is "Cain and Abel." Of course, we have to be careful in giving titles to Bible passages. They are of pure human origin, and, as such, have more to do with interpretation than with biblical truths. "Fall into sin," "original sin": both are theological terms and they should not influence the text. The text should remain an open source for ecclesiastical pronouncements.

If we want to be consistent, when we head Genesis 4 with "Cain and Abel," then the previous chapter should bear the title "Adam and Eve and the Snake," because that is the story there. And Genesis is a story. It is, as Martin Buber has said, *erzählte Lehre,* that is, instruction in story-form.

Thus, if Genesis 3 is "The First Sin," then logic dictates that the Cain and Abel story is "The Second Sin," and so on. We then would consider Abel's murder to be one of the many millions of sins we, the people who live after Genesis 3, continuously commit. The trouble with such a view is that it tends to create the impression that the sins in these two chapters are basically different from other sins, or perhaps constitute various stages in sinning. But that's not the case: we deal here in Genesis 3 and 4 with the one same basic source of evil and death, the very cause of all sin: our broken relationship with God. If we insist on adding titles to these chapters, it would be more appropriate to use "The Fall into Sin" for Genesis 3 and "The Economic Problem" for chapter 4.

Such titles would indicate why the two chapters form a unity — the third chapter in the Bible provides the theological basis for the fourth. Genesis 3 deals with "original sin," a concept many people nowadays see as belonging to another age. Indeed, take the case of that minister who, while trying to explain one of these confessional documents, expressed his belief that everything in this world is tainted with sin, even the newborn baby, whose crying he saw as an expression of covetousness! No wonder that many consider the teaching about sin a remnant of obsolete religious pessimism. But that minister was imposing his own interpretation on these passages. We must not forget that when the church teaches that we "are unable to do good and inclined to all evil," after the comma it continues, "unless we are born again by the Spirit of God."

Having spent six years in Latin America, from 1975 until 1981, I have discovered how realistic this reflection on original sin is. It makes real sense to take the message of Genesis 3 seriously and to affirm its deep insight into the human condition. How else can we explain the fact that, in the name of progress and development, millions of people in what we call the Third World have been inhumanely and cynically driven to death through the imposition of Northern systems and policies on the Global South?

How else can we explain, other than through original sin, the disappearance of tens of thousands of people in Argentina during the military dictatorship and the torture of even more? What other explanation is there than the message of Genesis 3 for the blasphemy of the totalitarian state which idolizes its own superiority and displays its power through violence and through the destruction of the very basic fabric of life? How else to explain the obliteration of the means of existence of an entire nation than by the omnipresence of original sin? (To top it all, these monstrous acts in Argentina were often instigated by faithful churchgoers.)

Still we maintain that we live in "the free world," that same Western world which in the 1970s and 1980s equipped and instructed the murderous regimes in South America and elsewhere according to the Western ideology of progress. Our economic textbooks usually open with the question, "What is responsible for the order in society?" And the answer is, "The market." But where is the proof? When we look at the world-market in its entirety, including the countries at the fringes, rather than observing order and life we see chaos and death.

Can all this really be separated from Genesis 3 and 4? After all, our Western economic institutions are products of human nature and claim to reflect the essence of what it means to be human. Do they in reality not reflect the ecclesiastical confession that we are unable to do any good and inclined toward all evil? Isn't it true that we are conceived and born in a society that's falling apart everywhere? Is it too far-fetched to say that we live in a world fixated with death?

We don't have to look far afield to find the victims of our economic system; Europe has them by the score and so does the United States of America. We see them not only in the old-age homes, but also in the alienated young people who will never have meaningful employment.

There are today people who put the blame for all this misery on the leaders of large business enterprises. They want to directly accuse these leaders of the death and destruction that happened in the Third World under their watch. A Reformed minister in North America once told me that we should go to New York and confront the CEOs of the large multinationals with the call to repent. According to him, these entrepreneurs would then cease to be exploiters and stop taking advantage of poor nations.

Well, I'll be the first to engage these business leaders in an extensive discussion, but a call to "repentance" sounds rather naïve to me, and the conclusion of this clergyman even more so. I believe it would be incorrect and also not quite honest to personally hold the leaders of multinational enterprises responsible for the chaos in international economic activity. None of them intentionally seeks to bring death and destruction to the developing world by means of economic activities. They are no murderers, certainly not intentionally. Even though we see the disastrous effects the economic system can have on the well-being of poor countries, we cannot simply blame businessmen. They will, for that matter, say: I can do no otherwise. My exports must go up. My market share must not go down. Competition forces me.

Who, then, are the culprits? We all are responsible. Not only businessmen — who, for all we know, may have the best intentions — but all of us participate in a coercive economic system based on growth, progress, security, expansion, the ever greater desire for more. It's all of us — the poor excluded, of course. It is clear that in the economy the question of death and life concerns all of us. Of course, business leaders and politicians are ultimately responsible for their actions. But we will all be called to account.

But let us return to Genesis 4. Until the story of Cain, death was unknown — and the text does not tell us that Cain intended to kill his brother. In the biblical revelation, death enters into human history as an unintentional, unpremeditated act. Listen to what the Apostle John writes about Cain. He says that Cain killed his brother "because his works were evil." Martin Buber has something to say about this as well. When he comments on the words "and killed him," he writes that "Cain did not kill Abel, but it turns out that he has killed him." Likewise, we don't kill others, but our actions accomplish it just the same.

"Can I help it?" Cain then asks. Imagine if you accidentally dropped a precious piece of china. The owner might say, rather annoyed: "What did you do now?" You might say, "I'm sorry — I just touched it, and boom, it shattered. I couldn't help it. I never noticed that it was in such a dangerous place. I did not put it there." The real problem in this case would be your attitude of disregard, not your specific action. In the same way God asks Cain, "What did you do now?" A murder has been committed. Not just one of the many millions in history. Here it concerns the sum of all murders, the biblical vision of murder. God says: "The voice of your brother's blood is calling to me from the ground." In the original Hebrew, the "blood" that is crying out loud to God is in the plural. Likewise, Matthew 23:35 speaks of "all the righteous blood shed on earth." This blood keeps on clamoring even today. (Indeed, a journal co-sponsored by Cardinal Arns of São Paulo carried the name *Clamor.* It was devoted to reporting the thousand-fold murders in dictatorial South America, especially in Argentina, Chile, Uruguay, and Bolivia. The heading on that paper was from Psalm 88:2, "Turn your ear to my cry.")

Two matters are striking here. First, Abel's death is not a spontaneous event. It is the consequence of something — the consequence of something being drastically amiss between Cain and God. The problem in Cain's relationship with God had consequences for Abel, just as our economic behavior has consequences, or "external effects," for other people. And of course, we must remember that groups as well as individuals can have the attitude of Cain; this is poignantly illustrated in a poem by an Argentinean mother whose son was killed by the military. She refers to the military system as Cain, recognizing that those whose "faces are fallen" (Gen. 4:6) as Cain's was can easily become functionaries in a faceless system. (More on that in the next chapter.)

In the second place, it is striking that Cain is portrayed as participating in a higher level of economic development than Abel. Cain is a farmer, while Abel is a shepherd. Yet rather than taking a protecting role as he should have, "as a guardian cherub" with outstretching shielding wings (Ezek. 28:14), he views Abel as a competitor. Cain shuts his heart to God and so, necessarily, to his brother also. The Apostle John says, "How does God's love abide in anyone who has the world's goods and sees a brother or sister in need and yet refuses to help?" (1 John 3:17). The mandate for humanity "from the beginning" was to love one another (1 John 3:11). This was the word of creation, the word of Life. Cain does not bother about the Word of God; he wants to stand alone. That's why "God's love cannot abide in him."

CHAPTER 4

A Military-Economic Security System

"And now you are cursed from the ground, which has opened its mouth to receive your brother's blood from your hand. When you till the ground, it will no longer yield to you its strength; you will be a fugitive and a wanderer on the earth." Cain said to the LORD, "My punishment is greater than I can bear! Today you have driven me away from the soil, and I shall be hidden from your face; I shall be a fugitive and a wanderer on the earth, and anyone who meets me may kill me." Then the LORD said to him, "Not so! Whoever kills Cain will suffer a sevenfold vengeance." And the LORD put a mark on Cain, so that no one who came upon him would kill him. Then Cain went away from the presence of the LORD, and settled in the land of Nod, east of Eden.

Cain knew his wife and she conceived and bore Enoch; and he built a city, and named it Enoch after his son Enoch.

GENESIS 4:11-17

In the previous chapter I noted that Cain can be viewed not only as a character in a biblical story, but also as a system. Likewise, the attack on Abel is not only that particular murder, but also represents the biblical vision of murder. Cain personifies the human attitude hostile to God, and in the same way, the "great city" in the Bible is not merely a collection of houses surrounded by a wall; it is a spiritual power.

Hostility toward God is called unbelief in the Bible, and Cain is the first to display it. "By faith Abel offered God a more acceptable sacrifice than Cain's," says Hebrews 11:4. Likewise, Matthew 23:35 calls Abel righteous because of his faith. Cain, on the other hand, wants to demonstrate by his works that he is righteous. He reasons that his sacrifice, which God found unacceptable, is in fact much better than his brother's. His rationale is that his offering is more genuine because he has invested time and trouble; he has done some real economic planning. Abel, by contrast, has no such pretensions. He is not righteous because of something he has done, or because of something in him, or because of some aspect of his character. He is set right with God "out of faith," that is, out of the recognition of God's free grace. Jacques Ellul, the well-known French theologian and philosopher, points at the beginning of his book *The Meaning of the City* to the difference between Cain and Abel. He notes that God reads Cain's hostility on his face, and in fact confronts him about it.[1] But Cain is not interested in mending his relationship with God. The result is his brother's death, an event after which God no longer addresses Cain in terms of a warning, but rather in terms of punishment. For Cain has cut ties with God and with his brother. Severing his connection with God also means that his connection to nature and to the world will be broken: "A fugitive and wanderer shall you be on the earth. . . . [The earth] will no longer yield to you its strength."

This calls for some economic reflection. In current economics textbooks, little emphasis is placed on relationship or concern for fellow human beings. Students are not taught that economics is an inter-human affair, that the primary dangers lie in repression and subjection and in pushing for economic domination. Rather, they are taught that the primary problem is scarcity, the fundamental shortfall of prosperity, which is to be diminished by means of technical progress through the greater application of individual economic calculation. Scarcity is presented as a phenomenon inherent in creation rather than the result of our lack of respect for God's Word and for the life of our fellow human beings.

The oppressed are always "righteous" vis-à-vis our relationship with God. Thus the sixteenth-century Spanish theologian Bartolomé de las Casas (1474-1566), a forerunner of contemporary liberation theology, described the native South American people as "perfect human beings,"

---

1. Jacques Ellul, *The Meaning of the City*, trans. Dennis Pardee (Grand Rapids: Eerdmans, 1970).

without evil intentions or pretense. He observed that the Christians — that is, the Spaniards — behaved like cruel wolves and tigers toward these "kind-hearted sheep." Indeed, "[they had] more regard for animals, even for the dung on the city squares" than for the native South Americans. Such an attitude could not help but result in widespread genocide, for "the ultimate purpose of the Christians was the gold. They wanted to fill their pockets with a maximum of treasures in the shortest possible time."

Christians always must, before pointing the finger at others' injustices, look at themselves and at the societal structures for which they are co-responsible. Paul himself writes, "I am the greatest of all sinners." Thus it is neither fashion nor emotion that drives me to state that we must look at our economic system through the eyes of the poor, from the point of view of the victim. Nor is it an impossible task. God himself is on the side of such people, for God hears the cry of the blood of victims of economic expansion. Oppressors may try to refuse to permit their systems to be measured with this yardstick; they would prefer that those who would cry out against them would be obliterated. Yet Abel, who was childless, who seemed eradicated, "died, but through his faith he still speaks" (Heb. 11:4).

When people build cities, they pass on and perpetuate injustice and the structures of oppression. Yet Abel is unable to transmit the righteousness that, according to Ellul, "is nothing more than the act by which God accepts his sacrifice."[2] Nevertheless, Abel acted keeping his eye on God, and so his sacrifice had God's approval, in an echo of God's approval of his good creation in Genesis 1. And it is because Abel lived in total dependence on the creation Word that he continues to live, even though he has been killed.

And Cain? Cain, the arrogant murderer, realizes to his bewilderment that now that he has abandoned the Word of God, he can no longer count on God's protecting presence: "I shall be hidden from your face; I shall be a fugitive and a wanderer on the earth." Cain, the killer, who has attacked somebody else, has imperiled the life of a man and caused his death, is now the one who is being confronted with the issue of safety. Security has become the problem for the perpetrator of violence himself. So in recent times when the Latin American military discussed "national security," it did not mean security for the poor and oppressed, but rather its own safekeeping and self-preservation.

Thus Cain has become an alien on the earth, estranged from the very

2. Ellul, *Meaning of the City*.

earth out of which he was formed. The earth is no longer faithful to him. Although it has been entrusted to him, he has abused this connection as well, defiling the earth through shedding his brother's blood upon it. In this sense a third party is implicated in the event. And God expresses his concern about the earth, its plants and animals. The earth, cursed because of the human race, corrupted by them, "vomits out its inhabitants" (Lev. 18:25). And this is where the economic problem originates: it is a human product, a direct consequence of the fall into sin, which led to ignoring the Word and to manslaughter.

Yet God addresses himself to Cain a third time. After warning and punishment comes an offer of protection: "And the LORD put a mark on Cain, so that no one who came upon him would kill him." But even now Cain does not believe; he doesn't rely on this Word. He fails to react, just as he failed to respond when God asked him why he was angry and why he asked his brother Abel to go to the field. He turns his back on the Word: "But Cain went out from the face of the LORD." (Some translations use the word "then" rather than "but" to begin this verse; however, the former does not convey the full force of Cain's negative reaction to God's offer.)

Cain goes out from the face of the Lord to live in the land of Nod, which literally means "the land of wandering." Thus it has remained ever since: the human person has become a stranger, unable to find the shalom that existed in Eden, restless, with nowhere to lay his head, alienated from nature, and feeling a lack of security. Nevertheless God invites human beings, burdened as they are, to live within the context of his promise. Cain is the human being fallen into sin: there is a schism between Word and world. Yet when God calls him to a risky trust in his promise, he refuses.

Cain instead goes to live "east of Eden." He chooses a new point of departure, one with important symbolic meaning. Focusing on the paradise he has lost, he sires a son and builds a city. He settles down. By these acts he renounces his status as an alien and the judgment implied therein. Both the son and the city bear the same name: Enoch, which means "inauguration" or "initiation." After God's beginning in Genesis 1 now follows Cain's "anti-beginning" of Genesis 4. Cain chooses to safeguard his own future through his offspring, and through his own economic and military security system: the city. The city is his answer to the economic problems (the earth no longer producing to capacity) and security problems ("whoever sees me shall kill me") besetting him. And so he walks away again from the creation Word, starting his own anti-creation. As Ellul puts it,

[Cain] wants to find an answer to a self-inflicted predicament, but he can never find it, because the solution depends on God's grace. Cain tries remedy upon remedy and each one means a new level of disobedience, a new curse. Each remedy, seemingly an answer to one of Cain's needs, in reality makes him sink even deeper into woe, into an ever more inextricable quagmire.[3]

I should note that when we talk about "the city" in this context, that is, as a spiritual attitude, we cannot automatically contrast it with the country-side. Our modern countryside has long since become an economic and cultural part of the city. Agriculture has grown into an industry that, in many cases, exploits and injures nature just as much as any other. Never-theless, the origin and rise of the city as such has to do with the rise of a ruling class that uses others to produce their food supply. This is the reason why the city is the cause of military and economic oppression, and why the countryside is dependent on the city in this sense.

"Anyone who sees me shall kill me," Cain exclaims. The thought of the other fills him with anxiety; he neither has nor needs a brother any longer. Recall that Robinson Crusoe, in the novel that bears his name, is gripped with panic at the discovery of some other person's footprints on the island where he has landed. Not joy at the thought that his lonely existence has ended, but fear! In this, Crusoe personifies the self-satisfaction that is all too common among the Western bourgeois: he sees the other, rather than himself, as an alien. That other turns out to be a black person whom Cru-soe knows only as "Friday" and who becomes a subservient or dependent in his economic system. The city enters the biblical narrative because of Cain's fears, a man-made construction founded on mistrust and an erro-neous sense of eternity.

One of the most influential ideologues connected with Latin Ameri-can militarism, the Brazilian general Golbery do Couto e Silva, based his vision of humanity on fear. Believing in the eternal insecurity of the hu-man race, he proposed as an answer for Latin America the "national secu-rity state." Likewise Milton Friedman, the well-known advocate of pure capitalism, observes outside the city of the free market system only tyr-anny, slavery, and misery. For him, the capitalist market economy must form the answer to human anxiety, loneliness, and insecurity.

3. Ellul, *Meaning of the City*.

Human beings who flee the Word desire to re-conquer paradise, to decide for themselves what is good and what is evil, and to subject the entire creation to their autonomous will. Their economic and military systems serve as a "second nature," a substitute creation, a new cosmos under human authority. But any such authority can only oppress. Each step on the way of progress after this anti-start of Genesis 4 can only mean a new level of disobedience, thus rendering the security problem — both economic and military — more inextricable.

CHAPTER 5

Technical Progress

*And they said to one another, "Come let us make bricks, and burn
them thoroughly." And they had brick for stone and bitumen for
mortar. Then they said, "Come, let us build ourselves a city, and a
tower with its top in the heavens, and let us make a name for ourselves; otherwise we shall be scattered abroad upon the face of the
whole earth." The* LORD *came down to see the city and the tower,
which mortals had built. And the* LORD *said, "Look, they are one
people, and they have all one language; and this is only the beginning of what they will do; nothing that they propose to do will now
be impossible for them. Come, let us go down, and confuse their language there, so that they will not understand one another's speech."
So the* LORD *scattered them abroad from there over the face of all the
earth, and they left off building the city.*

GENESIS 11:3-8

I have argued thus far that Christians, if they are really serious about
tackling economic problems, cannot merely define them in current "autonomous" terms. If they do, sooner or later they will find that they have,
after all, succumbed to assimilation and conformity with the world. Yet
when they come to their senses, before the face of God, they will be able to
distance themselves from the world's logic and their hearts' inclination.
Conversion, after all, is liberation — we saw as much in Chapter 1 with the
case of David and the three heroes.

Further, we cannot blame creation ordinances for the state of things, nor can we fault nature or unavoidable circumstances, as current economic thinking might suggest we do. All these are inherent in human history and are our human responsibility. Commercial activity and violence are interrelated; Ezekiel 28 and Genesis 4:8-10 remind us of that. The latter passage reveals that the real economic question is simply, "Am I my brother's keeper?" Cain's positioning himself against God through the manner in which he arranges his life and economy is what results in Abel's death. His question is meant to suggest that the outcome would have been different if only Abel had been more careful.

So again we see that the economic problem is really a spiritual matter; at its root is Cain's attitude of enmity toward God. This spiritual or religious character comes into focus especially in our security policies, for our security problems are truly the result of our own bad consciences and our own violent actions. Thus Cain builds a city in which he protects himself and in which he assures himself a place in history: it isn't good enough for him to guarantee that his name will live on through his children. In addition to Enoch the son comes Enoch the city, the economic-military security system that embodies Cain's defiance of God.

In this chapter I want to elaborate on the inner nature of the city's economy. The story of the city runs through the entire Bible, from beginning to end. Essentially it is the story of humanity following the example of Cain rather than Abel, searching for power and looking for worldly security.

After Cain, the next city-builder is Nimrod, the first man on earth to become a mighty warrior (Gen. 10:8). Nimrod is the son of Cush, who is the son of Ham, who was cursed by God — so again we see that the building of the city is the response to a curse. What was Ham's sin? When his father, Noah, had passed out naked from drinking too much wine, Ham came, observed his father, and reported to his brothers what he had seen. According to Jewish biblical scholar F. Weinreb, Ham typifies the realist, the developer, the progressive person, for whom a fact is a fact. Ham's brothers, Shem and Japheth, by contrast, go beyond what the eye notices, aware that such a view is limited. The report Ham gives is therefore deceptive, and his brothers respond to it by going to cover their father's nakedness.

Nimrod, Ham's descendant, is described as "a formidable hunter before the face of the LORD." Ellul suggests that the phrase "before the face of the LORD" means that Nimrod is a ferocious plunderer and conqueror, a user of indiscriminate force.[1] Genesis 10:10-12 lists several cities founded by Nimrod, so he is clearly an instigator of economic development, a nation-builder. He is a follower in Cain's footsteps. Further, most of the names of the cities he is reported to have founded appear repeatedly in the Bible, highlighting their symbolic significance as enemies of Israel's religion and as the places to which Israel is exiled.

Indeed, the name of one city, Resen, literally means "bit," that is, the part of the bridle that governs the horse. A bridled horse means civilization, power, and military strength of the kind that was always a spiritual as well as physical threat to Israel. Ellul describes Resen as the starting point of "the fantastic history of man which begins with the horse and leads to the splitting of the atom."[2] The biblical writers understood well that technical development and increasing armament are intimately related. (It is said that nearly half our Western technological research directly benefits the military sector.) Horses are weapons, and Israel is not permitted to put her trust in them: her king "must not acquire many horses," for to do so would inevitably lead to oppression by the city economy, the logical result of militarization (Deut. 17:16).

Nimrod's empire building and economic development takes place in the land of Shinar, which means "destroyer." It is amazing how destruction so often accompanies economic development, especially in our times! Richard G. Wilkinson wrote in the early 1970s that economic development from the Industrial Revolution and through the colonial period can be fully explained through the emergence of ecological problems which made a continual shift to new geographic locations necessary.[3] The current poverty of northeast Brazil can be traced directly back to the destruction of the environment by seventeenth-century Dutch sugar growers there. Further, the violence of the state in Chile, Argentina, Uruguay, and Bolivia in the 1970s and 1980s caused within a few years the total collapse of those nations' economies. For example, in Argentina the average wage dropped by 75 percent between March 1976 (the date of the coup) and July 1982.

Shinar is also the place where the Tower of Babel was built. We tend to remember this story mainly for the confusion of languages which took

1. Jacques Ellul, *The Meaning of the City*, trans. Dennis Pardee (Grand Rapids: Eerdmans, 1970).

2. Ellul, *Meaning of the City*.

3. Richard G. Wilkinson, *Poverty and Progress: An Ecological Model of Economic Development* (London: Methuen, 1973).

place there, but above all it is a story of the continuation of the building of the city. In it we see how the city — which was then an independent state as well — set its own economic policies, all with the goal of expansion. Babel is not, therefore, simply a tower. It is a city with a tower — therefore a military stronghold. Its fortifications foreshadow the walls that reached to heaven which so impressed and frightened the spies sent to scout the land of Canaan (Deut. 1:28, 9:1).

We are dealing, therefore, with another new beginning in the East. It is like Cain's, except the emphasis is on economic organization and technical progress. Three times the word "construct" appears. In the construction of large buildings bricks were needed; in the ancient Near East they were obtained through a system of mass production that relied heavily on the countryside. The translation of the Jewish Publication Society puts it well: "'Come, let us make bricks and burn them hard.' — Brick served them as stone, and bitumen served them as mortar — ." The people of Babel used bitumen rather than loam and bricks rather than stone: here we see what economists call the substitution of raw materials as a result of technical progress. Historical sources indicate that their economy would have been based on forced labor carried out by slaves deported from conquered countries and by laborers conscripted from the countryside.

Such a production process cannot be carried out without a political structure based on the threat of the sword, which in turn depends on a certain production scheme and a certain kind of product, for politics and economics are inseparable. The people of Babel sought to build a city, to set up a society that would be bounded by a closed ideological system and marked by progress. The Lord said: "this is only the beginning of what they will do; nothing that they propose to do will now be impossible for them." This, of course, is part of the ideology of progress, the desire to "make a name for ourselves" (Gen. 11:4). Those in power legislate what is truth. George Orwell in his novel *1984* illustrates in horrendous detail how truth can be robbed of its vehicle, language, as the state devises a means of expression which robs the people of the possibility to communicate and investigate.

Let us now turn to deal with the judgment the Bible pronounces on the city, even though it is already evident here: the story of the building of the city of Babel ends with the direct intervention of God. "Come," says God, "let us go down and confuse their language." God was not present in that city that had made a name for itself. From on high he descended, "and they left off building the city."

CHAPTER 6

Militarization and Oppression

So Jeroboam and the people came to Rehoboam the third day, as the king had said, "Come to me on the third day." The king answered them harshly. King Rehoboam rejected the advice of the older men; he spoke to them in accordance with the advice of the young men, "My father made your yoke heavy, but I will add to it; my father disciplined you with whips, but I will discipline you with scorpions." So the king did not listen to the people, because it was a turn of affairs brought about by God so that the LORD might fulfill his word, which he had spoken to Ahijah the Shilonite to Jeroboam the son of Nebat.

When all Israel saw that the king would not listen to them, the people answered the king.

> *"What share do we have in David?*
> *We have no inheritance in the son of Jesse.*
> *Each of you to your tents, O Israel!*
> *Look now to your own house, O David."*

So all Israel departed to their tents.

2 CHRONICLES 10:12-16

The above passage recounts how Israel as a nation was split apart, fulfilling a prophecy by the prophet Ahijah to King Jeroboam in 1 Kings 11:29-40. Israel reaches the pinnacle of its economic and political power during Solomon's reign, but it is a pinnacle achieved through extensive cooperation with the kings of neighboring lands. Solomon takes their political, military, and economic systems as a model, even going so far as to adopt their religions. This is what prompts Ahijah's visit to Jeroboam, who will soon become king over ten of Israel's twelve tribes.

Here again we are confronted with biblical thought on economics and politics; what may be most striking is how intrinsically intertwined the two entities are, given how we are accustomed to thinking of them as unconnected. Indeed, there are those who think that politicians should stay out of economic matters as much as possible. Often such a point of view is grounded in "science." Yet this faith in science is itself a political and economic statement, and it is contradicted by Christian social thought, which maintains that politics and economics are connected by their responsibility to protect the weak.

Solomon begins a program of international cooperation and economic expansion that is without precedent in Israel's history. First he builds the Temple, dedicating it himself with the pious prayer recorded in 1 Kings 8. (One has to wonder whether it is simple naïveté that leads him to have it designed by Canaanite architects, thus bringing elements of pagan culture into the center of Israel's religion.) After that seven-year project, he devotes a further thirteen years to the construction of his own palace complex, which includes government offices as well as an estate for his Egyptian wife. Under his leadership Israel becomes an international trading power, in league with Hiram, the Phoenician king of Tyre, a nation which we encountered in Chapter 2 of this book. In the harbor of Ezion-Geber Solomon obtains a seaport, with the result that he acquires a direct commercial link with the Indian Ocean (1 Kings 9:26). Historians surmise that this development may be the reason for the famous visit to Solomon by the Queen of Sheba: she may have seen her share in the Arabian caravan trade threatened by this joint venture of Israel and Phoenicia (1 Kings 10:2).

But Solomon goes even further than this. He addresses the security issue, thereby calling into question the very relationship between God and Israel. He closes the gap in the city wall of Jerusalem (1 Kings 11:27), and then undertakes a multi-year program of city-building, fortifying the nation with cavalry and chariots. All this in spite of the warnings to Israel's kings not to keep many horses, lest they come to resemble the oppressive Egyptian kings. It speaks volumes that Solomon begins his city-building boom with the reconstruction of the city of Gezer, which was the Egyptian king's dowry for his daughter when she married Solomon.

This kind of military buildup cannot be accomplished without the use of slave labor, which would have been drawn from the people of conquered nations (1 Kings 9:21). Yet some Israelites would no doubt have been conscripted as well — particularly those from the poor lower classes. First Kings 5:13 states that 30,000 men were engaged in forced labor in order to make Solomon's economic miracles possible; comparing this to the corresponding share of the American labor market today, we might envision 10 *million* people at work on these projects. In addition to these, some 80,000 men worked in the stone quarries and another 70,000 worked as common carriers. And there would have had to be several thousands of foremen and supervisors. In this way the class system is introduced in Israel, and the exploitation it entails is the leading reason for the appearance of Israel's prophets.

Solomon's wealth and his imperial policies fundamentally undermine the prior unpretentious structure of Israel's agriculture economy, causing for the first time the emergence of enormous wealth alongside crushing poverty and enslavement. This new societal structure is a direct result of Solomon's extensive defense expansion, which is in turn the reason for the prophet's condemnation. Solomon has put greater trust in military might than in the Lord's promises, and the result is a popular revolution against Solomon's son and successor Rehoboam, under the leadership of God's appointed Jeroboam.

Jeroboam leads the people of Israel to the new king, Rehoboam (2 Chron. 10:3). The people say, "Your father made our yoke heavy. Now therefore lighten the hard service of your father and his heavy yoke that he placed on us, and we will serve you." But the king listens to the counsel of "the young men," those who did not want to jeopardize their opportunities in the new societal system Solomon has established (1 Kings 9:22). In doing so, he forces all Israel to commit civil disobedience: "We have no share in David. Each of you to your tents, O Israel!"

In the meantime, the people remain in a state of confusion. The old ways of community and the former national unity are destroyed. God's covenant is broken, and to compensate for this rupture the people in their turn build fortified cities. Thus a new unity is forged: the people are behind the same walls, with the same weapons, all equally frightened, all wearing the same "uniform," all enslaved by the same ideology.[1]

---

1. Jacques Ellul, *The Meaning of the City*, trans. Dennis Pardee (Grand Rapids: Eerdmans, 1970).

Rather than relying on God's election, Rehoboam relies on his own power: "When he grew strong, he abandoned the law of the LORD, and all Israel with him" (2 Chron. 12:1). Being united in fear against the enemy, whoever the enemy may be, replaces the old unity that came from the fear of the Lord. Thus the people become victims of their own militarization policies. The king of Israel is elected to live by grace alone. When he relies on his own power, it is proper that he is defeated, even if he is fighting to defend the Temple.[2] And indeed, the Temple is eventually sacked by Shishak, the king of Egypt (2 Chron. 12:9).

All this should lead us to reflect on the military defense of our Western, "Christian" civilization. Militarization and economic injustice are strongly related to power politics. Neo-liberalism aims to separate economics from politics, following the political advice of Machiavelli, who famously proclaimed that it is better to be feared than to be loved. Yet the Bible contradicts this in the wise counsel given to Rehoboam by his elderly advisers, formerly in Solomon's service: "If you will be kind to this people and please them, and speak good words to them, then they will be your servants forever" (2 Chron. 10:7).

2. Ellul, *The Meaning of the City.*

35

CHAPTER 7

Development and Liberation

After this I saw another angel coming down from heaven, having great authority; and the earth was made bright with his splendor. He called out with a mighty voice, "Fallen, fallen is Babylon the great! It has become a dwelling place of demons, a haunt of every foul and hateful bird, a haunt of every foul and hateful beast. For all the nations have drunk of the wine of the wrath of her fornication, and the kings of the earth have committed fornication with her, and the merchants of the earth have grown rich from the power of her luxury."

Then I heard another voice from heaven saying, "Come out of her, my people, so that you do not take part in her sins, and so that you do not share in her plagues."

REVELATION 18:1-4

After this I heard what seemed to be the loud voice of a great multitude in heaven, saying, "Hallelujah! Salvation and glory and power to our God, for his judgments are true and just; he has judged the great whore who corrupted the earth with her fornication, and he has avenged on her the blood of his servants."

REVELATION 19:1-2

W e have so far been discussing the economic and technical development of "the city" in the Bible. This is not, of course, the holy city or the New Jerusalem of Revelation 21, but rather the human city: the city of Cain, of Nimrod, of the Israelite kings. It is the city represented by Resen in Genesis 10:11 and by Nineveh in the Book of Jonah, the "exultant city that lived secure, that said to itself, 'I am, and there is no one else'" in Zephaniah 2:15.

Revelation 18 relates God's final judgment on this city. It is a judgment that is inescapable, for where human beings may undergo conversion or repentance, the city cannot. In the Bible, God speaks to humanity in a different way than he addresses the city. The latter, as we have seen, is a kind of anti-creation, an artificial habitat to which people flee from God's Word, a seductive prostitute. It has forced the human race into a state of confinement, compelling them to follow its ways: humankind, seeking to ensure its own freedom by building its own stronghold, is ironically enslaved by the product of its own hands.

We do not always recognize this city in our own society, but it is there all the same, pervading the global world community. Fortunately there are still pockets of freedom and humaneness, but the simple fact is that most of our material prosperity is inseparable from the oppressive structure of the city described here. It is easy to be fooled by its beautiful appearance, to hear "the sound of harpists and minstrels and of flutists and trumpeters," the hum of the mill, the activity of the artisans — but not to hear "the blood of prophets and of saints and of all who have been slaughtered on earth" (Rev. 18:22, 24).

The Argentinean Nobel Peace Prize winner, Adolfo Pérez Esquivel, remarked during a visit to the Netherlands in the 1980s that Latin America had become the land of martyrs. Yet when he asked politicians there and elsewhere in Europe, and in the United States as well, why they sent so much weaponry to Latin American dictators whose blind quest for power resulted in bloodbaths and genocide, he always received the same answer: "If we don't sell them weapons, someone else will." In other words, "Am I my brother's keeper?" We live in a democracy; we cannot prevent what our business leaders do. We can't limit our arms production; it would lead to more unemployment. These and other responses like them all say, in essence, "The system forces us." They lead to an astonishing discovery: we are not free! We are cornered. If we don't comply with the system, our competitors will reap the benefits. This, indeed, is what the Great City is all about:

its own importance. The city becomes divine: "Apart from me there is nobody" (Zeph. 2:15). Its laws, economic and otherwise, are unconditional. Business is business. Whatever opportunities will benefit it automatically have priority. Consider the list of goods in Revelation 18:11-13: gold, silver, and precious stones at the top; grains, livestock, and *human lives* at the bottom. The lives of human beings are the city's least valuable commodity. Indeed, today we have developed neutron bombs that can destroy human lives without harming buildings and goods.

There is only one way to be freed from this system: escape. God orders his people to flee, as Lot from Sodom (Gen. 19:17). For simply by living in the city we participate in its evil, in its curse. The city leaves us no alternative but to sin (Rev. 18:4). It forces all its inhabitants into bondage. "Come out of her," Revelation 18 tells us, "so that you do not share in her plagues" — lest you perish in her judgment, as befell the German families in Dresden at the end of World War II, the innumerable Lebanese in Beirut in 1982, and the Iraqis in Baghdad in 2006.

Today more than ever we as Christians must determine our position vis-à-vis the city, the godless military-industrial complex that churns out its lethal products regardless of who is being killed as long as the killing happens somewhere far away. It is not only a matter for really committed "church people" who are always involving themselves in Christian actions; nor is it only for those who like to specialize in being critical of society. It is a matter that concerns all Christians. It is central to our faith. If we do not know what is going on in this world, how can we grasp the meaning of Jesus' words, "I have overcome the world" (John 16:33)?

Yet to come out of the city does not mean to abandon the world to its own devices, to retreat to our cabin in the woods, or to have our own "green" job or special project or cause, like Jonah did when he constructed his own little booth away from Nineveh to observe the destruction of the godless (Jon. 4:5). Nineveh, after all, the city, is the world in which we live. We cannot be mere observers. To the contrary, God has elected us for a purpose: to go to Nineveh and bring the Good News.

This requires a continuous effort on our part to discover where Nineveh is located, to find the borderline between church and world. Has the world invaded the church? Is the Spirit at work in hidden places in Nineveh, as she was in Jonah's day, and to his dismay? We can be certain that the city is found wherever people are encouraged to seek only their own financial benefit, even when this is done in the name of the greater good — "individual selfishness creates harmony for all." For the export of arms has taught us that exactly the opposite is true: these lethal products (or indeed, any products) may end up in the wrong hands and cause great destruction despite the individual virtuous laborer or the individual good manager who produces them. Even our good intentions and well-meaning acts, thanks to the logic of the city, may become agents for injustice, death, and devastation.

All this puts into perspective Cain's question, "Am I my brother's keeper?" Dutch poet Huub Oosterhuis puts it this way: "To forces we surrendered, to more than our own blame." The city is just such a force. We tend to think of sin in individual terms, as emanating from individual hearts, but the city seduces the hearts of even the just, forcing them to participate in injustice. "If anyone put a stumbling block before one of these little ones," says Jesus, "it would be better for him if a great millstone were fastened around his neck and he were drowned in the depth of the sea" (Matt. 18:6). This is precisely why God will obliterate the city.

Only God can deliver us from the city. It is not a matter of development, but of liberation. Our citizenship in heaven, which we already possess (Phil. 3:20), allows us to live in the earthly city and to work there as if we were nonresidents. We must prophesy against the war machine while praying for the city and seeking her peace (Jer. 29:7). In coming chapters we will explore ways in which we can live on the basis of the expectation of the New Jerusalem, the holy city to come. "Let the same mind be in you that was in Christ Jesus" (Phil. 2:5) means that our discipleship cannot be divorced from our economic life.

PART III

SIGNPOSTS

CHAPTER 8

The Economics of Honor

*Honor your father and your mother so that your days may be long in
the land that the LORD your God is giving you.*

EXODUS 20:12 (NIV)

*The Pharisees and scribes came to Jesus from Jerusalem and said,
"Why do your disciples break the tradition of the elders? For they do
not wash their hands before they eat." He answered them, "And why
do you break the commandment of God for the sake of your tradition? For God said, 'Honor your father and your mother,' and 'Whoever speaks evil of father or mother must surely die. But you say that
whoever tells father and mother, 'Whatever support you might have
had from me is given to God,' then that person need not honor the father. So, for the sake of your tradition, you make void the word of
God. You hypocrites! Isaiah prophesied rightly about you when he
said: 'This people honors me with their lips, but their hearts are far
from me; in vain do they worship me, teaching human precepts as
doctrines.'"*

MATTHEW 15:1-9

It may seem counterintuitive to connect the fifth commandment with
economics. Both in church and in the home, this commandment has
historically been used to support parental authority. It is about obedience,

43

rule, submission. It has a parallel in Romans 13, "Let every person be subject to the governing authorities."

It is not my intention here to claim that the fifth commandment has nothing to do with authority. But it should be clear by now that the nature of this authority must not be identified with the secular society that surrounds us. Unfortunately, all too often Christians, both Protestants and Catholics, have interpreted these passages in exactly this way. For example R. H. Tawney, the famous economic historian, demonstrated that the typical Protestant concept of authority has closely paralleled that of the dominant economic system of that time.[1] With the rise of the modern wage economy, both church and state emphasized the authority of the father (supported by the mother) as breadwinner: when the father comes home, tired from his important work, he must not be bothered with trivialities.

Of course, parents in ancient Israel, just like parents in every other nation, exercised authority over their children. Indeed, for children to obey their parents was so important that Deuteronomy 21 prescribes the death penalty for children who refuse to listen to their father or mother, and Exodus 21 prescribes it for children who strike either parent. (The Talmud indicates that this penalty was rarely carried out; it merely served as deterrent and warning.) With such a cultural emphasis on parental authority, however, why would it be necessary to enshrine it in the Ten Commandments? The only explanation is that the essential meaning of the fifth commandment lies elsewhere.

The Ten Commandments are traditionally divided in two: the first five teach us the proper attitude toward God, while the second five teach us the proper attitude toward our neighbor. The first tablet is about loving God; the second is about loving neighbor. The two decrees, to love God and to love neighbor, are equal (Matt. 22:39); to quote the apostle John, "Whoever does not love, does not know God. . . . Those who say, 'I love God,' and hate their brothers or sisters, are liars; for those who do not love a brother or sister whom they have seen, cannot love God whom they have not seen" (1 John 4:8, 20). And Jesus teaches that in order to love God we must love our fellow human beings, preferably the lowest and most miserable among them (Matt. 25:31-46).

I would argue that the fifth commandment serves as a link between

1. R. H. Tawney, *Religion and the Rise of Capitalism: A Historical Study* (New York: Harcourt, 1937).

the first and second tablets. The deep secret, the mystery contained in "honor your father and mother," lies in the fact that parents are the medium for relating the great deeds of God to their children. It is up to them to make God known; they act for God. Interestingly, the fifth commandment is also the only one of the Ten Commandments that does not contain any prohibition, any "you shall not."

God chooses his people, not vice versa. In the same way, children do not choose their parents. And just as God calls his children by name, so parents call their children by name. They are name-givers. We human beings do not name ourselves — the sin of Babel consisted in doing just that. When John writes that love for God, who cannot be seen, must be recognized in the love we display toward the people we do see, then parents are an important link in this chain of love, since they are literally the first people we see in life. Our parents, our fathers and mothers, are, before anyone else, our neighbors.

What is the economic significance of all this? Perhaps surprisingly, the very core of this commandment lies in its economic meaning. It is precisely — and without any activity whatsoever on our part — in father and mother that we are confronted with the neighbor as the messenger of the God who is the author of authority. The people of Israel were forbidden by God to deprive the nonproductive, the weak, the invalids, and the aged of their rightful dignity and honor. It was usual in surrounding desert societies to abandon old people and let them die in places outside their settlements — a practice that may still be found today. Exodus 21:17 states, "Whoever curses father or mother shall be put to death." While we tend to think of cursing as uttering a malediction against someone, in this context it is better envisioned as leaving someone alone in his or her misery, as the meaning of the Hebrew root is "to rob persons of what is theirs."

Jesus employs this word in Matthew 15 when debating with the Pharisees regarding economic assistance for aging parents. According to Matthew, the Pharisees essentially place service to God in competition with service to parents, arguing that making a charitable donation to the church trumps using that same money to help parents in dire straits. Yet this way of thinking plays the first half of the Ten Commandments against the second, and Jesus sees right through it: these Pharisees, for all their piety, are hypocrites, professing to love a God they cannot see while ignoring the needs of their all-too-visible parents. Their religion has become sterile; their tradition has degenerated into human ordinances. Their hearts are not accessible, inquiring after neither God nor the neighbor — and in the biblical view, that shuts them off from both God and neighbor.

It is impossible to remain filled with the love of God when we fail to help a brother or sister in need, when we close off our heart to their suffering (1 John 3:17). If we have managed to earn a living in this world, if we can make ends meet, then we ought to put our life on the line for that brother or sister. Indeed, Christian thinking on economic matters is moving away from the familiar growth-based model and toward one "beyond poverty and affluence," to borrow the title of a recent important book on the subject.[2] Such a model contends that there is enough for all. And it is only when we are deeply concerned about those who are suffering that we can honor God in our economics. The fifth commandment has everything to do with economic matters. It is in economics that it becomes apparent whether we have spiritualized the Great Commandment — that is, to love God above all — or whether we have recognized it to be of equal value to the second — that is, to love our neighbor as ourselves.

2. Bob Goudzwaard and Harry de Lange, *Beyond Poverty and Affluence: Toward an Economy of Care* (Grand Rapids: Eerdmans, 1995).

CHAPTER 9

Productivity and Justice

Unless the LORD builds the house,
  those who build it labor in vain.
Unless the LORD guards the city,
  the guard keeps watch in vain.
It is vain that you rise up early,
  and go late to rest,
eating the bread of anxious toil;
  for he gives sleep to his beloved.
Sons are indeed a heritage from the LORD,
  the fruit of the womb a reward.

PSALM 127:1-3

And why do you worry about clothing? Consider the lilies of the field, how they grow; they neither toil nor spin, yet I tell you, even Solomon in all his glory was not clothed like one of these. . . . Therefore do not worry saying, "What will we eat?" or "What will we drink?" or "What will we wear?" For it is the Gentiles who strive for all these things; and indeed your heavenly Father knows that you need all these things. But strive first for the kingdom of God and his righteousness, and all these things will be given to you as well.

MATTHEW 6:28-29, 31-33

I n the previous chapter we saw that the fifth commandment teaches us to accept our responsibility for the weak and for those who have been placed in our life's path. This is in contrast with the current global economic system, whose orientation is wholly toward the market. And while the market favors the strong, the Bible portrays God as standing in solidarity with the poor and the weak. The Jewish thinker Emmanuel Levinas writes that the neighbor is God's associate, God's ally, and the voice of the neighbor in need is a voice from on high.[1] Our neighbors in need speak God's language to us in the same way that in Israel parents spoke God's language to their children.

Some might wonder whether this economic interpretation of the fifth commandment is materialistic or reductive in some way. Yet the real problem is that for far too long we have spiritualized the Bible, severing the first tablet of the law (which deals with loving God) from the second (which deals with loving the neighbor). Listen to Levinas:

> The spirit of the Jewish Bible is grounded in the reality that the connection to the Divine travels via the connection to humans and coincides with social justice. Moses and the prophets are not concerned with the immortality of the soul: they are concerned with looking after the poor, the widow, the orphan and the stranger. The tie to our fellow humans, which is the key to the Divine, is not some sort of "spiritual friendship," but a friendship that is expressed, proved and perfected in a just economy. And every individual person bears full responsibility in this matter. When a Roman citizen asked Rabbi Akiba, "Why doesn't your God, who is the God of the poor, feed those poor people?" the Rabbi replied, "To keep us from escaping damnation." There is no stronger way to express the impossibility for God to assume the duties and responsibilities that do belong to the human race.[2]

The poor, the unfortunate, are there for the sake of our salvation! As God's associates, they bless us. Perhaps you have had the experience of giving a beggar some money — thinking all the while that he will only use it to feed his addiction to alcohol. Yet when that beggar said, "God bless you," he

---

1. Emmanuel Levinas, *Difficult Freedom: Essays on Judaism,* trans. Sean Hand (Baltimore: Johns Hopkins University Press, 1990).

2. Levinas, *Difficult Freedom.*

spoke as one of the least of Jesus' brothers (Matt. 25:31). That relationship with Jesus gave him the authority to pronounce just such a blessing.

Once when I was living in Buenos Aires my doorbell rang and I opened the door to the sight of an old woman. She asked me for some water to help her swallow her medicine. "I never ask for money," she said, "even though I have nobody in the world. My only son, who was a lawyer, has died. I do ask for something to eat and to drink." When I had made some tea and we started a conversation, I asked how she managed to stay alive. She replied, "If God feeds the birds in the heavens, will he not look after me?" Here was a poor woman who spoke God's language! I had heard many missionaries using similar words, preaching sermons based on Jesus' words in Matthew 6, but none of them ever rang true. I realized then that only those who are poor themselves can speak with any authority about the state of being poor, because to the poor belongs the kingdom of heaven. A new Spanish translation of the Bible puts it this way: "Blessed are those who choose to be poor, for they have God as their king" (Matt. 5:3). John Calvin, the Reformation theologian, also singles out the poor as those who must, in Jesus' place, instruct the rulers of the church. Liberation theology refers to this as "the church of the poor."

There is no question that this biblical view differs vastly from the dominant modern view. In current economic thinking the poor are at the margins, not the center. Productivity is at the center, and the poor may be given a handout if there is enough surplus after we have made sure we have all the latest technology. A few nations have political parties and other groups who are trying to change this, but on the whole the world goes along with the Dutch banker who is reported to have said, "We have nothing to gain from helping underdeveloped areas. Our country will need every penny to keep up with technical development." Time and again we hear that we had better stop talking about the alleviation of poverty through international aid policies, that we had better learn to adopt a "no-nonsense attitude" or a "realistic view." This follows the advice of Adam Smith, who in his *Wealth of Nations* wrote that "a man must be totally insane if he does not invest all the capital at his disposal."[3] And even before Smith an English Puritan writer concluded that a person must only love another person as far as common sense allows, so that there was time left to love God! In other words, not too much neighborly love, because that would harm our love for God! What a contrast to what the Bible teaches us!

3. Adam Smith, *The Wealth of Nations* (New York: Modern Library, 2000).

Solomon's pilgrim song, Psalm 127, reads, "If the LORD does not build the house, in vain do its builders labor." (Martin Buber translates it by saying that its builders "labor under a delusion.") It goes on to say that an individual's children are his or her reward (the word here means the same as wage or salary) — not any money we may earn in order to bequeath it to them, but the children themselves! Children are an inheritance of the Lord in order that the fifth commandment may be implemented, the decree of the economics of honor. This is indeed a radical teaching in our current economic system.

The great economist John Maynard Keynes (1883-1946) identified the sickness that stems from our obsession with efficiency, which forces us to sacrifice for posterity. He noted that rather than enjoying the leisure that our pet cats delight in, we tend to look at cats as a means to breed more kittens, who, in turn, are also a means to breed more kittens, and so on. Thus we feel compelled to organize our future.[4] Contrast this with the Bible, where God simply provides us with "all these things as well" (Matt. 6:33). When we put the fifth commandment and the economics of honor into practice, then "our days will be long." This points to a state of prosperity where life itself is the central point, where time gains in quality and meaning. Yet we cannot attain this state by conquest. We will only enjoy it as the Promised Land "that the LORD your God will give you" (Exod. 20:12).

Jesus' Sermon on the Mount, in which he speaks of the birds of heaven and the lilies of the field, includes the line "Give us this day our daily bread." How absurd these words must seem to modern economists! To them, any bread we have is the reward for our own productive investment strategies. But what exactly does Jesus mean? The latest New Testament scholarship suggests that it may be better to render this text "Give us today our bread for tomorrow." This is extremely clarifying, for of course our heavenly Father knows that we need bread on a daily basis. But living with the Word, on the way to the kingdom, means being secure in our knowledge of the promise of the future. That's what the Lord's Prayer is about, after all: the coming of the kingdom, when we no longer have to "toil for the bread we eat" (Ps. 127:2), but where bread and wine will be given to all according to their need. We can live today without worry because we have been promised our bread for tomorrow. In this view, the Sermon on the Mount is truly a pilgrim's song.

4. John Maynard Keynes, "Economic Possibilities for Our Grand-Children," in *Essays in Persuasion* (New York: Norton, 1963).

CHAPTER 10

The Missionary Community

When it was evening, the disciples came to him and said, "This is a deserted place and the hour is now late; send the crowds away so that they may go into the villages and buy food for themselves." Jesus said to them, "They need not go away; you give them something to eat."

Then Jesus called his disciples to him and said, "I have compassion for the crowd, because they have been with me now for three days and have nothing to eat; and I do not want to send them away hungry, for they might faint on the way."

When the disciples reached the other side, they had forgotten to bring any bread. Jesus said to them, "Watch out, and beware of the yeast of the Pharisees and Sadducees. They said to one another, "It is because we have brought no bread." And becoming aware of it, Jesus said, "You of little faith, why are you talking about having no bread? Do you still not perceive? Do you not remember the five loaves for the five thousand, and how many baskets you gathered? Or the seven loaves for the four thousand, and how many baskets you gathered? How could you fail to perceive that I was not speaking about bread? Beware of the yeast of the Pharisees and Sadducees!"

MATTHEW 14:15-16; 15:32; 16:5-11

51

B oth Mark and Matthew relate two incidences of a miraculous feeding. Superficial commentators have dismissed this as repetition, perhaps with the goal of emphasis on the part of the evangelists. Yet if we carefully read Matthew 14–15 and Mark 6–8, it becomes clear that we are not dealing with repetition, but with something much more important.

Of course, we are dealing once again with economics and our daily bread. In the last chapter we raised the question whether the issue of bread is materialistic, but in the Bible it never is. Bread always points to the one who gives it. Consider the words of Martin Luther:

> When you talk about your daily bread and pray for it, then you pray also for everything needed to obtain the daily bread and also how to enjoy it. You also pray to be spared from anything that prevents bread from coming your way. That's why you must be open minded and take the next step, not only asking for the direct means, such as the oven or the flour, but embrace the entire picture, the field where the wheat grows, and the whole wide world that provides us with the daily bread and all other food products as well. After all, if God did not allow it to grow, would withhold his blessing and so prevent it from growing to maturity, we would never be able to take a loaf out of the oven and put it on the table.

This "miraculous feeding" (a term which, incidentally, may be popular among commentators but is never used in the Bible itself), too, is entirely a spiritual matter. The way we treat our daily bread — the matter in which we share or hoard it — always has a spiritual basis. Bread is more than simply a basic foodstuff. Indeed, Jesus goes so far as to identify the kingdom of God with a meal of bread (Luke 14:15). Both here and in the Lord's Supper Jesus teaches his disciples to exercise community, to enter into a communion of which he is the head. He himself gives the instructions; he makes it possible for the disciples to divide the bread in such a way that everyone present has enough, just as those who hunger and thirst for righteousness will be satisfied (Matt. 5:6). We see here the fullness of God's creative power.

Many commentators point out that the five loaves and two fishes in these stories symbolize the five books of Moses and the two stone tablets of the Law. Thus the Word of God is the basis upon which the disciples stand, and from it they are able to distribute. Likewise, the five thousand people symbolize all Israel, who will have life in abundance if they feed on the books of Moses and the Law. And the twelve leftover baskets stand for the Twelve tribes of Israel.

All this is fine as far as it goes, but in the messianic community, the one willing to be instructed and healed by Jesus' word, we must go deeper. We must give due recognition to the material aspect of the narrative. The Gospel writers do not neglect it. When the large crowds stay with Jesus as the day wanes, the disciples grow nervous and want to send them away to do what would be perfectly normal: to buy some food from local merchants before closing time.

Yet it is at just this point that Jesus begins to teach. How do we acquire bread? Certainly not by listening to a sermon and then sending everyone on their way! That's no way to host a gathering! When the disciples in their amazement ask where food enough for thousands of people will come from, Jesus points out that sharing comes before production. The exercise of community — that is, equitable distribution — is the source of prosperity, not vice versa. It is not that there are first twelve hampers full of leftovers out of which everyone may take a scrap of food; first there is the sharing, fully expecting that faith will see us through. The twelve hampers are the fruit of exercising the economy of sharing.

What is the source of this sharing? Not the "forces of production" unfastened from nature by "private property." To the contrary, its source is God's grace. Like a Jewish father, Jesus takes the bread, offers a prayer of thanksgiving over it, and hands out pieces to all who are seated at the meal. In this way no one is shortchanged, and the material abundance that remains is not a goal toward which all must sacrifice their daily existence, but rather a gift of grace granted "as well," when, day by day, our life is focused on seeking the righteousness of God's kingdom and geared toward listening to Jesus' teaching.

Here the meaning of the Gospels vis-à-vis our modern economy is made plain in no uncertain terms. Everything in our current economic system aims at increased productivity, at growth rather than the ability to share. It's impossible to feed the world's population, goes our current wisdom, unless we first give a free hand to multinational enterprise with its enormous potential for production. More output means more wealth, which will allow for more handouts. (Churches are often seen as requiring such "handouts." Production precedes religion. When representatives of the Dutch Council of Churches approached an organization of business

leaders several years ago to draw their attention to the need for just investment practices, one of the businessmen retorted, "You would not be able
to engage in this dialogue if we had not provided you with your daily bread
— that's how you have the leisure to discuss politics with us!") Yet the
Gospels teach us that the only solution to world hunger is to share first.

A recent report of the New Economics Foundation, entitled *Growth
Isn't Working,* states that the world's total available biocapacity consists of
11.5 billion hectares of biologically productive space — grassland, crop-
land, forests, fisheries, and wetlands. Thus on average there are 1.8 hectares
of "environmental space" per person. Yet the average European requires
4.7 hectares to produce the resources she consumes and to absorb the
waste she generates. Given that the European Union only has 2.3 hectares
available per person, the rest of its footprint falls with a thud outside Europe's borders. And the use of global hectares per person is twice as much
in the United States as it is in Europe. Too, the ecological burden exerted
per person has grown much more quickly in high-income countries than
it has in developing countries. The "footprint" per person in wealthy nations grew from 3.8 global hectares in 1961 to 6.4 in 2001 — an overall increase of 68 percent. In developing countries, the increase over the same
period was just 7 percent, from 1.4 global hectares per person to 1.5 — indeed, it actually *fell* between 1981 and 2001.[1]

The report concludes that we should not be evaluating economic policies based on whether they aim to maximize total income, and hope for
poverty reduction as a byproduct; but rather on whether they specifically
increase the incomes of poorer households and treat growth (or the lack of
it) as a byproduct. After all, global economic growth is an extremely inefficient way of achieving poverty reduction — and it is becoming even more
so. Between 1990 and 2001, for every $100 worth of extra global production
and consumption in the world's per person income, just $0.60 found its
"pro-poor" target and contributed to reducing poverty below the $1-a-day
line. And this tiny benefit was offset by enormous negative impacts on the
environment.

In Latin America, as in so many Third World countries, land redistribution and other large-scale land reform are fundamental prerequisites for

---

1. David Woodward and Andrew Simms, *Growth Isn't Working: The Unbalanced Distri-
butions of Benefits and Costs from Economic Growth* (London: New Economics Foundation,
2006).

economic development and justice. Only when this is the primary objective can all other things be given as well (Matt. 6:33). When it is not, the result is continuous oppression by police and army, whose strong-arm tactics keep unjust regimes in power.

The community of Christ is concerned with care for the neighbor. In that crowd of five thousand, not a single person is asked whether he is adhering to the ordinances of the current system, such as the edict not to eat with unwashed hands (Matt. 15:2, 20). It is up to the church today to put Jesus' alternative into practice. We may call the multiplying of the loaves a miracle, but for Jesus it was something quite consistent with the logic of the kingdom of God.

The second "miraculous feeding" takes place in pagan territory, in the Greek region of Decapolis (Mark 7:31). Here the disciples find themselves in a "mission field" — a crucial test. Will they be concerned with the plight of the people, or will they trip up again on their own impotence or unwillingness, cloaked in the glib question, Isn't it time for the people to go find something to eat? In Matthew 15 it is entirely up to Jesus to take the initiative; this second time the disciples don't even pose the question. The crowd, outside Israel's territory, has been with Jesus for three days, immersed in his teaching and healing. Jesus calls his disciples together to wonder what should be done next. Apparently the disciples have totally forgotten about the previous feeding; or perhaps they reason that something like that should only take place within Israel's borders. At any rate, Jesus teaches something different: now there are four thousand mouths to feed, symbolic of the four winds, thus the entire world. And there are seven baskets left over, representing perfection and the presence of God.

There is more at stake here than mere bread. This is why Jesus adds a warning, his third, against "the yeast of the Pharisees and the Sadducees," the persecutors of the church. Mark relates that the disciples had forgotten to take bread along on this journey: had they learned a lesson? Or were they primarily concerned with their own needs? This is how they interpret Jesus' warning about the yeast. The fact is that their anxiety needs to take a completely different direction. The yeast so hostile to Jesus pervades all of society: it penetrates the reigning societal system by giving both religion and politics a different spiritual outlook. "Then they understood that he had not told them to beware of the yeast of bread, but of the teaching of the Pharisees and Sadducees" (Matthew 16:12).

CHAPTER 11

The Real Treasure Is Friendship

Then Jesus said to the disciples, "There was a rich man who had a manager, and charges were brought to him that this man was squandering his property. So he summoned him and said to him, 'What is this that I hear about you? Give me an accounting of your management, because you cannot be my manager any longer.' Then the manager said to himself, 'What will I do, now that my master is taking the position away from me? I am not strong enough to dig, and I am ashamed to beg. I have decided what to do, so that, when I am dismissed as manager, people may welcome me into their homes.' So, summoning his master's debtors one by one, he asked the first, 'How much do you owe my master?' He answered, 'A hundred jugs of olive oil.' He said to him, 'Take your bill, sit down quickly, and make it fifty.' Then he asked another, 'And how much do you owe?' He replied, 'A hundred containers of wheat.' He said to him, 'Take your bill and make it eighty.' And his master commended the dishonest manager because he acted shrewdly; for the children of this age are more shrewd in dealing with their own generation than are the children of light. And I tell you, make friends for yourselves by means of dishonest wealth, so that when it is gone, they may welcome you into the eternal homes."

LUKE 16:1-9

56

F inally, here we have a text about a genuine economic matter! There is a lord who, as the Greek has it, employs an "economist," someone who manages his estates. Apparently this lord hardly ever takes the trouble to look in on his own financial affairs, leaving it all up to his manager. Perhaps he is a city dweller, just as some families in Spain still have their haciendas in Mexico. In any case, all he cares about is that the bank balance stays out of the red. Yet someone, we don't know who, tips him off to the fact that his manager is engaging in financial improprieties. This administrator has hitherto enjoyed a good position. In the economic system of his day he occupies a place of relative power that in all likelihood offers security for the future. Indeed, he must have been counting on such security, for he has no idea how he will support himself now that he is about to be dismissed.

The standard interpretation of this parable, particularly in Protestant circles, is that the manager gets out of his predicament by falsifying certain IOUs, reducing one debtor's debt by half, and another by 20 percent. Thus it is often referred to as the parable of the "unjust steward," because the manager depreciates the value of something belonging to his master, thereby buying the goodwill of certain debtors who will later express their gratitude by supporting him.

The latter part of this interpretation is correct — but the fact is that we have no reason to believe that the manager falsifies any documents. Rather, he simply cancels an injustice done by the creditor to the debtor. In other words, he does nothing more than renounce the interest that he had intended to charge the farmers for his own gain, a common practice in spite of the Jewish law prohibiting usury. Lenders would not calculate interest separately, but add it instead to the principal (moneylenders in developing countries today use similar practices). Thus a sum of 50 was borrowed, and 100 was required for repayment — amounting in effect to 100 percent interest, or more if the term was less than one year. Or again, 25 percent interest on a loan of 80 adds up to 100. These high rates, and indeed higher ones, occur quite frequently in situations like this — after all, the borrower needs seeds and his daily bread, and being in dire straits he has little alternative but to accept the offer of the usurer, hoping that he can repay it out of the proceeds of the coming harvest. It is obvious within this context that the friends this steward makes are poor people; it is equally clear that the interest revenue has been obtained fraudulently.

Jesus is quite outspoken here: those who try to advance themselves in the money economy will sooner or later have to resort to unjust methods. The Greek word used in verse 9 for "wealth" is *Mammon*. Mammon is a false god, a personification of greed or avarice; worship of Mammon is, by definition, intimately linked with injustice. We have to face the fact that economists who refuse to admit that money is "eminent desire" and who don't consider the social realities behind it, mistaking the veil of money for the real economy, are themselves economists of injustice. We simply cannot accept an easy treatment of stewardship that bypasses the fall into sin of Genesis 3.[1] For with respect to the handling of money, we are all economists of injustice. To be rich is never a matter of neutrality. Stewardship may be a pious and well-intentioned theory, at best derived from a paternalism supposedly based on divine right, but in reality it may serve only to justify the possession of unjust riches.

The biblical mandate, on the other hand, centers precisely on how to deal with these ungodly and unfair matters. How to be faithful in such a system requires thinking against the grain, a skill we obtain from different treasures, those "that do not perish" (Matt. 6:19). How we deal with money determines how qualified we are to "be entrusted with true riches" (Luke 16:11). Money is defined as "what belongs to another" (Luke 16:12). Economic theory defines money as the power to dispose of the goods or services of others. If money takes on a life of its own and acts as an independent entity, then we are included in its built-in injustice. And so we, too, must be stewards of injustice, for that is where life in this framework of injustice intersects with the new life we have through faith in Jesus Christ. We cannot serve both God and Mammon, and so we can never rid ourselves of this money problem. We are called to demonstrate God's sovereignty over the possession of wealth, which is only possible through faith.

Those who think in terms of money and whose life is determined by money — economists of injustice, in other words — soon lose sight of the boundaries of the law. It's no surprise that the steward in this story broke the law against levying interest. Yet the fundamental question posed by this parable is this: how does human law relate to the law of God? Even though the Torah prohibited the charging of interest, the practice was widespread. The Pharisees, Jesus' ideological opponents, strictly obeyed the Torah, but they were money-hungry as well (Luke 16:14). So they devised a way out.

1. For more on this see Jacques Ellul, *Money and Power*, trans. LaVonne Neff (Downers Grove, Ill.: InterVarsity, 1984).

They reasoned as follows: God has prohibited the charging of interest in order to protect the poor from exploitation. So it is not allowable to obtain interest from a debtor by means of goods not accessible to him. But there is no objection to giving a loan and asking for interest on it in terms of goods that are handled by a debtor on a daily basis. Because in each household one can always find a bit of oil and a bit of wheat — they are, after all, daily needs — a loan agreement involving oil or wheat is not against the law.[2] In this manner they sought to obey the letter of the law while disregarding its spirit. It is this economic context to which Jesus refers when he talks about the impossibility of serving both God and Mammon (with its human-made law system). Jesus preaches faithfulness even in "the very little" (Luke 16:10; Matt. 25:21).

The interest he is charging amounts to a personal benefit for the steward, but he is wise enough to let go of it. This is what the parable is all about. Eugene Peterson, in his well-known *The Message*, entitles this passage "The Story of the Crooked Manager," and in that translation it culminates with the line, "The master praised the crooked manager, because he knew how to look after himself." However, this fails to do justice to what Luke wants to make plain here. In the first place, the passage is not about a crooked manager, but about an economist of injustice. He is not crooked, but simply a follower of usual practices. Nowhere does his master accuse him of new irregularities (even the wrongdoings mentioned in verse 2 are not mentioned again, as they have no relevance to the larger point). In the second place, the parable is not concerned with an instance of being "smart," some kind of success story. The manager is not "crafty" or "clever," but "wise," "prudent." He is wise because he seeks the solution to his problem outside the logic of the unjust economic system. He is wise not only because he makes amends, but also because he no longer relies on Mammon, but rather on the compassion of poor farmers. He repairs the human relations which had been obscured by the lust for money which, according to 1 Timothy 6:10, is the root of all evils. This is the kind of choice Luke labels wise.

The steward does not seek future security in a new accumulation of capital. (In all likelihood he had a nest egg tucked away from years of duping his master as well as from charging interest to his debtors.) Rather, he seeks it in acquiring friends. Of course there is an element of cunning in

---

2. J. Duncan and M. Derrett, *Law in the New Testament* (London, 1970).

this, but it is much more a sign of wisdom. The steward cannot have known that his actions would pay off; the deal was not watertight. Yet to Jesus he takes a more promising route. No longer are the farmers victims of exploitation. Rather, their former creditor has joined them in a new relationship, containing both the seeds of uncertainty and hope. The money that was first a cause for separation is now a tool for making friends. The Californian monetary economist Lietaer quotes John Perry Barlow as saying: "The economy of the future is based on relationships more than on possession."[3]

This friendly money is now no longer a source of temptation to acquire more and more, another step in the eternal pursuit of greater wealth. It has instead become a virtuous means to improve human relations. The manager has dethroned Mammon, the money god. He has deprived him of his holy status. Ellul puts it well: "That's how money has been returned to its simple role of material instrument. When money is not more than an object, when it has lost its tempting influence, and no longer has its high value, its superhuman dazzle, then we can utilize it as an ordinary tool."[4]

The master congratulates his fired administrator for acting sensibly; he would have done the same thing. And if the children of this world, the participants in a corrupt economic system, are capable among themselves to seek their mutual advantage, how much more must the children of light befriend each other! (When Jesus says "children of light," he is using a familiar Hebrew expression referring to those whose natural habitat is out in the open.) Jesus affirms that money must be used, but not according to its own logic. Even though money is unclean, tainted by lust and power, it can be used to achieve just human relationships. The poor with whom money can bring us into relationship will welcome us into the eternal homes. In the passages that follow this one, the rich man calls on poor Lazarus to bring him relief (Luke 16:24), the poor are said to represent Jesus (Matt. 25:31-46), and the kingdom of God is said to have the poor at its gate to welcome us (Luke 16:9).

We are all partners with unjust Mammon: the point is to remain faithful, especially in the small things that are in our reach and in which we can make a difference (Luke 16:10-12). The point is that the money that passes through our hands in our day-to-day economic transactions, if we really

3. Bernard Lietaer, *The Future of Money: A New Way to Create Wealth, Work, and a Wiser World.*

4. Ellul, *Money and Power.*

go to the bottom of it, actually belongs to somebody else — it is, as John Calvin points out, a blessing from God. This is the case even if we earn and spend money truthfully and responsibly, and even though the economic system, with all its built-in injustices, tends to resist large-scale change.

All this goes against the grain of liberal theory, which proclaims that what you have earned is yours — after all, you worked for it. Not so. Work must be meaningful in itself;[5] it must be done to the honor of God, to the benefit of our neighbor, and to the maintenance and expansion of a Christian lifestyle. When we live in this way, we discover that prosperity is not something we earn, but rather a gift. And well-being is not a matter of planning; Mammon may promise as much, but it does not deliver. All our actions should center on the restoration and conservation of human relations, even if they involve going against prevailing custom as in the case of the unjust steward. The ultimate authority, after all, rests with the Word of God, and of what is written there not a stroke of a letter will be dropped (Luke 16:17).

There are two ways: the way of God and the way of Mammon. We can have allegiance only to one. "No slave can serve two masters; for a slave will either hate the one and love the other, or be devoted to the one and despise the other. You cannot serve God and wealth" (Luke 16:13; Matt. 6:24). Abraham Kuyper puts it this way:

First pray to God as well as Mammon. Then the soul becomes as hard as iron, eradicating all religion. Finally not only does the worship of God disappear forever but something of the former worship emerges in a different form which then takes the shape of some sort of religious honoring of both money and Mammon. This is why there is no other possibility: if we don't sever the ties with Mammon, our allegiance to God will eventually die out. In the end, only service to Mammon will remain.[6]

To be faithful to God has not only to do with "spiritual" matters, but "should be written into the things of this world."[7] That's the reason why the children of the light also must consult together and act rationally.

---

5. Lietaer, *The Future of Money.*
6. A. Kuyper, *Pro Rege*, part I (Kampen: J. H. Kok, 1911).
7. Ellul, *Money and Power.*

CHAPTER 12

Population and Food Policies

Now a new king arose over Egypt, who did not know Joseph. He said to his people, "Look, the Israelite people are more numerous and more powerful than we. Come, let us deal shrewdly with them." . . .

The king of Egypt said to the Hebrew midwives, one of whom was named Shiphrah and the other Puah, "When you act as midwives to the Hebrew women, and see them on the birthstool, if it is a boy, kill him."

EXODUS 1:8-10, 15-16

If you see in a province the oppression of the poor and the violation of justice and right, do not be amazed at the matter; for the high official is watched by a higher, and there are yet higher ones over them.

ECCLESIASTES 5:8

The land shall not be sold in perpetuity, for the land is mine; with me you are but aliens and tenants.

LEVITICUS 25:23

R eading the above passage from Ecclesiastes may conjure up images of a police state wherein all people are viewed as acting suspiciously, and wherein one set of government employees is spied upon by a higher set, which in turn is watched by those of a still higher status. Such a picture may lead to the conclusion that it is solely the unwarranted use of power that results in the suppression of the poor and the violation of law and justice.

In fact, however, this text deals with the authority system itself, as the *Nueva Biblia Española* understands when it gives it the heading "Authorities." Numerous philosophers and theologians have recognized as well the problem posed by the authority system: Herman Dooyeweerd, for example, warned in the strongest possible terms against the absolute authority of the state (hence the concept of sphere sovereignty, in which the state is called upon to confine itself to its proper sphere of competence). Jacques Ellul also points out that the power of money as well as the power of the state are great threats to the Christian way of life. State socialism, with its widespread bureaucracy, is indeed a Mammon system, typified by totalitarian rule. People in this system must constantly compete to advance up the bureaucratic ladder — just as, of course, they must constantly compete in the free market system to advance up the ladder.

Any hierarchical national government, ruled from above, in which one layer of authority is overseen by another, and that one by yet another, is, as such, a danger to the poor and a cause of the miscarriage of justice. This passage from Ecclesiastes warns us — indeed the entire Bible warns us — against the indifferent government machinery that operates at the expense of those who depend upon it economically. We saw this earlier, in Chapters 4–6, in our discussion of the city and the tactics it employs to expand continuously at the expense of the countryside.

In light of this, some Bible translations go on to say that it is a good thing when there is a king who favors a plowed field, that is, the countryside, for such must be the best antidote to poverty and economic injustice. Other translations, however, wisely take into account a king's potential to be the origin of oppressive poverty: in that sense the economy of the entire nation is serving the political class! Thus the "alternate reading" contained in the Revised Standard Version is the most correct: "The profit of the land is among all of them; a cultivated field has a king" (see Chapter 15).

Yet land is not something to be pledged to higher powers who will grow rich by it. Land has been given to the human race as a means to make a living (Lev. 25:23). Some claim that the world's food problem is so large that we can manage it only by giving free rein to the efficiency of the dominant economic and political powers, to multinational enterprises and "no-

nonsense" governments. Yet the proponents of this approach ignore the causes of this drama. Our economic framework is such that even though agricultural production increases, it does little for the poor and for the right treatment of the soil. In the Third World, agriculture is geared more toward export, to promote the production of meat in the overfed West, and to grow the raw materials for alcohol distillation and other luxury purposes (to say nothing of the cultivation of drugs).

When the poor are driven off their land for the benefit of this sort of power system, as was the case in the infamous "model" settlements during the dictatorships in Guatemala and the Philippines, then we may indeed see agricultural production, but the development of the countryside to benefit those who live there is nonexistent. Official rural development policies are hardly ever concerned with the promotion of a healthy rural growth in which the true priority is to feed the local population.

Where, then, is the solution to the problem of sufficient food? It lies in implementing an "economy of sufficiency" for those who work the land and occupy it. Our present economy is not one of "enough," but of "more." What this means is that those with economic and military power are always pursuing, and receiving, more; while the poor receive less — or nothing at all. Our notion of "private property" is nothing but a front to rationalize Third World famine. Those multinationals, with their hundreds of millions of hectares as well as their local allies in the Third World who possess immense land holdings, can only sustain this system by keeping the peasants away from their possessions by force, and chasing them from their traditional homesteads. This is the reason why Roman Catholic bishops in Brazil have stated that we must distinguish between "private" ownership and "capitalistic" ownership: the latter is for the benefit of speculation, profit generation, and the maintenance of an economic power structure; the former promotes conditions where people can carve out a proper existence.

The Bible is unambiguous: "Cursed be anyone who moves a neighbor's boundary marker" (Deut. 27:17). Likewise, Isaiah says, "Ah, you who join house to house, who add field to field, until there is room for no one but you, and you are left to live alone in the midst of the land!" (5:8). And the prophet Amos condemns those who trample on the poor and abhor those who speak the truth and take from them levies of grain. That sort of power structure, Amos warns, will be destroyed (5:9-11).

The systematic moving of boundary markers was a feature of European life from the Middle Ages until the nineteenth century, as the enclosure of "commons" was carried out to provide a rising class of commercial agricultural entrepreneurs with greater expansion possibilities. The real victims of this practice were small growers and traditional landowners. As land was bought and sold, an economy of accumulation arose, and with it injustice in general. Animal husbandry became more lucrative than growing crops, leading Sir Thomas More (1478-1535) to state that "sheep swallowed people." This process of confiscation in the name of private property has been going on in the developing countries since colonial times; indeed it has gone into overdrive. Ecclesiastes' observations about authority are definitely true today.

There are some who would sell us a bill of goods about a global "population problem" in order to divert our attention from the global food problem and the widespread need for land reform. But the fiction of an overpopulated world is easily exposed as a myth. It is claimed that there are too many people because every new baby will use in its lifetime too many resources and cause too much pollution. The fact is that the claim a poor child makes on natural resources is nothing compared to that of an adult in the developed world: the real problem lies not with a newborn in South America or Africa, but rather with persons in North America and Western Europe. In her book *Sex and Destiny,* Germaine Greer sums up the problem with population politics:

> The blind conviction that we must meddle in the procreational behavior of others and perhaps, if necessary, act against their wishes in this matter, stems from the conception that the world belongs to us, the very people who very expertly have exhausted its resources, while not to those who have refrained from doing so.[1]

We don't need a population policy; we need a food- and land-distribution policy. We don't need the kind of rules made by the Pharaoh in Egypt who felt threatened by the demographic growth of the Israelites; we need the kind of rules that will put judicial assistance and land reform at the center of any program for development. Only when rural areas flourish will we find out how much room is left for the city. Only when the interest of the poorest of the poor is primary will the question of the First-World economy become important.

1. Germaine Greer, *Sex and Destiny: The Politics of Human Fertility* (New York: Harper & Row, 1984).

CHAPTER 13

Faith and Equality

Moses said to them, "It is the bread that the LORD *has given you to eat. This is what the* LORD *has commanded: 'Gather as much of it as each of you needs, an omer to a person according to the number of persons, all providing for those in their own tents.'" The Israelites did so, some gathering more, some less. But when they measured it with an omer, those who gathered much had nothing over, and those who gathered little had no shortage; they gathered as much as each of them needed.*

EXODUS 16:15-18

At the present time your plenty will supply what they need, so that in turn their plenty will supply what you need. The goal is equality, as it is written: "The one who gathered much did not have too much, and the one who gathered little did not have too little."

2 CORINTHIANS 8:14-15 (TNIV)

To everyone who conquers I will give some of the hidden manna, and I will give a white stone, and on the white stone is written a new name that no one knows except the one who receives it.

REVELATION 2:17

M any people shy away from relating the Bible to matters of political and economic significance. They recall the abuses of this process in ages past. Or they wonder, for instance, whether it is possible to apply texts written two or three millennia ago to our modern society, regardless of whether that society is capitalistic or socialistic. Besides, isn't biblical interpretation a very subjective affair, with each person interpreting texts in his or her own way? And why should a Christian religious book come to bear on both Christians and non-Christians? And aren't religious texts generally opposed to the compromise that is necessary to solve problems rationally?

Of course the Bible is not meant to provide easy answers for our day-to-day economic problems — not now, and not at any other time in human history. Nor is it merely an ethical handbook. The Bible is a message: it is the Word of God, in which God communicates about himself and about humanity, addressing himself to each individual man or woman with ears to hear. It is not a set of rules and regulations but a proclamation of grace, a call to trust and faith in the God who is the Father of Jesus Christ. And it is a warning against false gods who would lead humanity in different ways.

The relevance of this revelation has no limit, a notion which flies directly in the face of the modern scientific view that life must be compartmentalized. The Bible calls us to a service of God that embraces the totality of life. All we do, in word and deed — and that certainly includes professional labor and political activity — we must do in the name of the Lord Jesus (Col. 3:17). The commandment to "love the Lord your God with all your heart, and with all your soul, and with all your mind, and with all your strength" (Mark 12:30) fiercely disputes the tendency to separate Sunday from Monday, labor from leisure, idealism from realism, economy from ethics, ethics from faith, because "the Lord our God, the Lord is one" (Mark 12:29; Deut. 6:4). And it does not allow room for alibis or excuses along the lines of, "Oh, this field is not directly connected to the Bible."

The biblical call to faith and obedience is directed to each individual human being, not to some abstract idea of humanity. This latter kind of "spiritualizing" — which in fact is not spiritual at all — is the most cunning trick of the great enemy of the message. "Didn't God say . . . ?" So begins Satan, the deceiver, in his attempts to persuade Eve and Jesus that conformity to this world enjoys divine approval (Gen. 3:1; Matt. 4:1-11). In each case he follows up with a very straightforward Christian truth, but taken out of context so that only its letter, not its spirit, is available. In this way the critical sharpness that should form the hallmark of the Christian community is blunted, with the result that most Christians no longer "may discern what is the will of God — what is good and acceptable and perfect" (Rom. 12:2). Jesus overcomes the temptation in the desert by pointing to the great Old Testament commandment, reiterating the importance of knowingly serving a God who has nothing in common with the gods of surrounding nations (Matt. 4:10; Deut. 6:13-14).

That the Bible speaks not only to believers in the first century but to those in the twenty-first as well is not because its message stands outside time, but rather because its message teaches us how to understand the time in which we live. The same powers which in earlier times were active between God and humanity are still at work; only their outward manifestations have changed. The Bible teaches us to recognize these appearances for what they are. This is certainly true as regards economic matters, as well as the gigantism and militarization that plague our Western system. "The reality which the Bible reveals," says Jacques Ellul, "is in total agreement with what current secular thinking is able to show us. However, the Bible digs deeper and outlines the causes."[1]

In the previous two chapters we discussed two different powers: those of money and the state. These are the powers that compete with the liberating God of the Bible (Deut. 6:15). Each claims the human spirit for which God yearns jealously (James 4:5). Money is a source of seduction for the very reason that it is money — this ancient truth was known long before capitalism came along. Indeed, the Hebrew word for "money" is derived from a verb which means "to desire" or "to pine for something." Money is even more powerful when it becomes as intertwined as it has with the power of the state. The Bible is perceptive enough to personify it as Mammon, a false god. The Bible's depiction of money as a spiritual powerhouse is borne out when we analyze its role in society, from earliest times all the way up to the present. Yet the Bible is not a book of economic prescriptions. It is both deeper and broader than that — much to the dismay of economists who would securely compartmentalize their discipline.

The biblical norm for work, as I have already pointed out, is not governed by money. What we do in daily life should not be determined by the

---

1. Jacques Ellul, *Money and Power*, trans. LaVonne Neff (Downers Grove, Ill.: InterVarsity, 1984).

amount of money we make. To work is to operate within the framework and the liberty of the Great Commandment; it is a fundamental part of the engaging of all our intellect and all our physical strength to God's honor, serving our neighbor and caring for creation in order to "serve and protect it," as philosopher Martin Buber translates Genesis 2:1. Our remuneration is not an accomplishment in itself, but a blessing, something someone else has handed us from somewhere. When Paul contends that "anyone unwilling to work should not eat" (2 Thess. 3:10), he does not mean that we work in order to eat; he means that we need to work because there is work to do. Work is service to the community; whoever does not wish to be part of a community through work cannot expect food from that source. Paul says this in connection with his own unusual circumstances as a traveling apostle — he does not wish to create the impression that his office as apostle entitles him to avoid making a living. He wants to earn his own keep. Those who refuse to work he describes as "liv[ing] in idleness, mere busybodies" (2 Thess. 3:11). Work derives its value not from what it pays; it stands on its own. If work does not stand on its own, compensation does not redeem it. Our income is a gift, and this is why everyone is entitled to it, according to need.

How an economy regulates the matter of work and reward is a question that society and politics must solve. Here especially Christians need to be on their guard against the spiritual power of current dominant trends in economic thinking. Christians need to hear these words spoken by an African woman: "Economic thinking is only interested in producing food for money, for the market; but we depend on it for our lives and that process takes place for us in essence outside the market and not for an income. That's why there is famine in Africa."

When the Israelites received manna from above, they were presented with an exercise in thinking spiritually. They were given the opportunity to have trust, forbidden to hold extra, and permitted to gather as much as they truly needed. This, says Paul in 2 Corinthians, is how true economic equality emerges. Biblical equality is never uniformity or conformity; it is a matter of spirit, a question of faith.

Revelation says that those who prevail will receive the hidden manna. Jewish sources tell us that this text is a reference to a golden jar of manna which the prophet Jeremiah had hidden in a cave on Mt. Nebo after the destruction of the temple. This cave, it was said, would be rediscovered on the Day of the Lord. The writer of Revelation connects this hidden manna to the eventual victory of Jesus; partaking of this manna serves as a counterweight to eating the sacrificial meat mentioned in the letter to the congregation at Pergamum, that is, to participating in the system and making compromises (Rev. 2:12-17). Those who conquer will not be submerged in the anonymous mass of the modern economy in which one consumer is interchangeable with any other and one employee is as good as another. Those who conquer will be confirmed in their genuine personality, in their deep-seated relationship with him who will name them with a new name, which will remain secret between giver and receiver, written on a white stone, which is the admission ticket to the kingdom of Heaven.

CHAPTER 14

Risen above the Power of Money

Solomon had a vineyard in Baal-hamon; he entrusted the vineyard to keepers; each one was to bring for its fruit a thousand pieces of silver. My vineyard, my very own, is for myself; you, O Solomon, may have the thousand, and the keepers of the fruit two hundred.

SONG OF SOLOMON 8:11-12

Give me neither poverty nor riches; feed me with the food that I need, or I shall be full and deny you, and say, "Who is the LORD?" or I shall be poor, and steal, and profane the name of my God.

PROVERBS 30:8-9

I know what it is to have little, and I know what it is to have plenty. In any and all circumstances I have learned the secret of being well-fed and of going hungry, of having plenty and of being in need. I can do all things through him who strengthens me. In any case it was kind of you to share my distress. . . . I have been paid in full and have more than enough; I am fully satisfied, now that I have received from Epaphroditus the gifts you sent, a fragrant offering, a sacrifice acceptable and pleasing to God.

PHILIPPIANS 4:12-14, 18

71

I t is beyond argument that the Bible has opted for the poor. Latin American liberation theology is built around this fact; the Washington-based evangelical Jim Wallis has said that if we eliminated all references to the poor and the oppressed in the Bible, we would be left with a jumble of unrelated quotations without any context. The pursuit of wealth, whether individually or collectively, is a false goal, because the quest for money at all costs results in the stewardship of injustice that is condemned in Luke 16.

The Old and New Testaments speak in somewhat different voices about the problem of wealth: where the latter is more outspoken, the former is more nuanced. Ellul points out that wealth in the Old Testament can assume the character of a sacrament, as the abundance of the Promised Land is a sign of the coming of the New Creation, and as wealth shows the gratuitousness of God's election, which is not based on merit but on God's grace. Wealth, then, is a blessing that has no salutary meaning apart from our relation to God. "Solomon's wealth," he says, "is not necessarily similar to that of Standard Oil."[1] Wealth in the Bible has both prophetic and eschatological significance; it is an indication of what is to come in the New Jerusalem, into which the glory and the honor of the nations will be brought (Rev. 21:26). Wine and bread are the symbols of the coming kingdom; the request for bread in the Lord's Prayer appears there to remind us of the coming of that kingdom, as we discussed in Chapter 9. The possession of wealth has spiritual meaning. It is not an end in itself; its presence must not be confused with possession of God's blessing.

Thus in the Old Testament there are only a few righteous rich people — for example, Abraham, who has to abandon his comfortable existence in order to be blessed and to be a blessing, and Job, who undergoes a severe testing as Satan tries unsuccessfully to prove that his wealth is a matter of self-interest. But the real example of great riches in the Old Testament is Solomon; he becomes rich for the very reason that he has not asked for it:

> Because this was in your heart, and you have not asked for possessions, wealth, honor, or the life of those who hate you, and have not even asked for long life, but have asked for wisdom and knowledge for yourself that you may rule my people over whom I have made you king, wisdom and knowledge are granted to you. I will also give

1. Jacques Ellul, *Money and Power*, trans. LaVonne Neff (Downers Grove, Ill.: InterVarsity, 1984).

you riches, possessions, and honor, such as none of the kings had who were before you, and none after you shall have the like. (2 Chron. 1:11-12)

Yet Solomon, however proverbial his wealth remains, eventually forgets its source as well, and after his death his kingdom is divided and eventually exiled. Even the Song that bears his name recognizes that there are things which cannot be bought, things much more important than money. "Keep your treasures, Solomon," it says in effect. "My vineyard is free."

Milton Friedman, the great proponent of the modern market economy, has been the topic of much discussion in the economic-theological literature in Latin America. Friedman rejects in principle everything that would place a barrier between human beings and the exploitation of resources, for such barriers prevent free exchange between buyer and seller. In his various writings, he singles out agricultural programs, minimum wage legislation, labor laws, old-age income, and regulations governing the granting of licenses, to name but a few. Yet the theologian Franz Hinkelammert points out that under such a system as Friedman advocates, everything that makes human life livable in this world will be enclosed by the fence of a price, a cage with a lock that can only be opened by dropping a coin into a slot; it will become impossible for "the sun, a forest, or a park [to] be enjoyed without anybody paying for that pleasure."[2] There will be no more vineyards outside the market system. Friedman's strange vision of freedom as an infinite series of cages containing an infinite amount of goods has parallels with the South American juntas that wanted to see freedom in terms of an infinite number of army bases and the banning of communication and cultural endeavors that were not financed by or supportive of the military dictatorship. Both may bring to mind Orwell's *1984*, in which love itself is disallowed by the state.

Yet love, in Song of Solomon 8, is the road back to wisdom, away from the world of buying and selling, the world of acquisitions, profits, mergers, and expansion. This world, of course, is the great city, driven by violence and by a uniform ideology, whose merchants are the magnates of the earth who "deceive all nations by their sorcery" (Rev. 18:23). Greed drives them to deceit, to the "false words" of 2 Peter 2:3. It leads them to treating human

2. Franz Hinkelammert, *The Ideological Weapons of Death: A Theological Critique of Capitalism* (Maryknoll, N.Y.: Orbis, 1986).

beings like objects to be bought or sold; yet like Abel's blood the exploitation of the laborer cries out to God. "Listen, the wages of the laborers who mowed your fields, which you kept back by fraud, cry out, and the cries of the harvesters have reached the ears of the Lord of hosts. . . . You have condemned and murdered the righteous one, who does not resist you" (James 5:4-6). The economic problem is not merely a question of rich and poor; it is one of life and death, as we saw in our study of Genesis 4. Solomon's wisdom and piety were primarily the result of his refusal to demand the lives of those who hated him (2 Chron. 1:11). Wisdom always includes respect for life.

Economic violence contravenes the Christian teaching regarding the coming of the Lord. James condemns those who, while living in the end times, are just accumulating their riches. "You have laid up treasure for the last days" (James 5:3). Jesus points out that the servant who begins to mistreat his fellow servants or to engage in a self-indulgent lifestyle is clearly not expecting the imminent return of his master (Matt. 24:48-49). Such statements as these indicate that the Bible is primarily a book of faith, not a book of ethics. Ethics are derived from the knowledge and wisdom gained by faith. Indeed, the very sin of those who nail Jesus to the cross is that "they do not know what they are doing" (Luke 23:34). The author of Proverbs fears riches because they stifle knowledge; yet poverty, too, endangers the honoring of God. Thus he prays to be spared both poverty and wealth. This is important: poverty is not glorified. What is important is choosing what is just, as Leviticus 19:15 indicates when it says "you shall not be partial to the poor or defer to the great: with justice you shall judge your neighbor."

Neither poverty nor wealth is the ultimate reality; life is not exclusively about economics. It is the unfortunate fate of our time that everything seems to be forced into an economic straitjacket. Perhaps it's no longer possible to visualize the kind of world envisioned by Professor J. H. Boeke (1884-1956) of the University of Leiden. Working at the intersection of spirituality and economics, he cited how an Indonesian village was not primarily a work center, a place to produce things, but rather a retreat, designed for its inhabitants to relax in. Our current system is nothing like this; it makes life worse for both rich and poor. Mammon requires sacrifices from both camps.

Nevertheless, the rich are responsible for poverty (Ezek. 34:18-19). The Bible rarely shows an exception to the rule that the rich tend to become assimilated with their riches, making it harder for them to enter the kingdom of Heaven than for a camel to go through the eye of a needle (Luke 18:25). Some wealthy Christians bristle at such notions, at such so-called "leftist theology." They argue that the church should include all kinds of people, not just the poor. But it already does — for "what is impossible with human beings is possible with God" (Luke 18:27). What the rich need to remember is that their redemption, just like that of the poor, comes only from God. The imitation of Christ indeed follows the prayer of Proverbs 30. But it is no matter of steering a careful, middle-of-the-road course. Rather, life lived in Christ empowers everything, regardless of wealth or poverty, when both are stripped of their ability to enslave.

The apostle Paul had a particular economic relationship with the Christians in Philippi (Phil. 4:15). They financed his mission work. Yet the arrangement was not purely economic (2 Thess. 3:7-8). It had spiritual implications. "It was kind of you to share my distress," he writes (Phil. 4:14). Indirectly, this offers a critique of the kind of one-sided thankfulness that sometimes occurs in churches. There is thankfulness on both sides, Paul's and the church's, because "I seek the profit that accumulates to your account" (4:17). This account is of a spiritual nature. Assisting Paul was in fact an offering pleasing to God.

Judas, who sold Jesus (Matt. 26:15), did not like sacrifice. He considered the myrrh, that precious oil which the woman had poured on Jesus' head, a waste of good money. It could have, he points out, been turned into hard cash and distributed to the poor (Matt. 26:9). Jesus' disapproval of Judas's view on this matter proves that not all theology concerning the poor is biblical. (In the matter of what constitutes a proper sacrifice, Protestants often have an edge over Catholics in determining what is wasteful and unprofitable.) Christ is not a representative of the poor — such a view would rightly be labeled politicized theology. Rather, the opposite is true: the poor represent Christ (Matt. 25:31-46). The poor represent Christ not based on whether they are Christians, but simply because they are poor. This is the point Jesus, who personifies the bought-and-sold poor, wants to make to the rich, and it is as true today as it was then: "The poor you will always have with you" (Matt. 26:11). This is why the church cannot help but be a church for the poor — as not just the proponents of liberation theology but also great reformers such as John Calvin have pointed out.

To be wealthy is to be called to a high spiritual level. It is an invitation to bring fragrant and pleasing sacrifices out of solidarity with those who need us to share in their distress. In Christ all things are possible — even the dethroning and desacralizing of money and of the state. The manner by which money, as if by magic, is robbed of its power is through the gift, the transfer for which no return is asked. This is the way God works; as Ellul says, "The only way in which God behaves is the way of giving."[3] Likewise, the way by which the state loses its oppressive character is through justice. Countering the forces of possession (money) and oppression (the state) in our modern world means running against its very logic. In our society, the gift is suspect; its legal status is subject to a multitude of conditions. Yet for those trying to go against the grain, one simple rule of thumb is valid in our economic and political conduct: "Let each of you look not to your own interests, but to the interests of others" (Phil. 2:4).

Here it is helpful to remember the story of Jonah, which is both prophetic and educational. Jonah is chosen: God chooses him to speak the Word of God against Nineveh, the godless city (Jon. 1:2; 3:1-2). But like many prophets, Jonah objects to his assignment. He boards a freighter and flees in the opposite direction, away from Nineveh and toward Spain. Yet eventually, after a storm at sea and time spent in the belly of a great fish, Jonah acquiesces to God's will. He expresses God's judgment over the people of Nineveh. Against all odds, the inhabitants of the city repent, which leads God to spare the city.

The ending of Jonah's story is almost comical: the prophet, wishing to see his people's enemies destroyed, picks a fight with God over the fate of Nineveh. Having spoken his prophetic word, he retreats to a place outside the city, where he can observe what happens. In the sweltering heat, a tree miraculously grows, providing him shelter and shade. Yet it withers, and when it does, Jonah feels sorry for himself. Then comes God's reprimand: "You are concerned about the bush, for which you did not labor, and which you did not grow . . . should I not be concerned about Nineveh, that great city, in which there are more than 120,000 persons who do not know their right hand from their left, and also many animals?" (Jon. 4:10-11).

This question, the last great prophetic question in the Old Testament, reverberates through the rest of the Bible. And it is directed to us today as well. Those who don't know the difference, those who are ignorant, those who don't know what they are doing: those, says, God, I have decided to

---

3. Ellul, *Money and Power.*

save, even if you don't agree with it (Acts 3:17; Luke 23:34). The Book of Jonah ends without waiting for Jonah's response — God's word is final.

"Let each of you look not to your own interests, but to the interest of others." Some translations distort this simple truth by adding "not only" to the first statement, and "but also" to the second. Yet this is completely unwarranted and unnecessary. Paul's original words in Philippians 2 disclose the secret of understanding what the Bible proclaims about our economy as the place where faith and unbelief meet.

PART IV

Justice and Expectation

CHAPTER 15

Globalization

Again I saw all the oppressions that are practiced under the sun. Look, the tears of the oppressed — with no one to comfort them! On the side of the oppressors there was power — with no one to comfort them.

ECCLESIASTES 4:1

If you see the poor oppressed in a district, and justice and rights denied, do not be surprised at such things; for one official is eyed by a higher one, and over them are others higher still. The increase from the land is taken by all; the king himself profits from the fields.

ECCLESIASTES 5:8-9 (NIV)

All this I observed, applying my mind to all that is done under the sun, while one person exercises authority over another to the other's hurt.

Then I saw the wicked buried; they used to go in and out of the holy place, and were praised in the city where they had done such things. This is also vanity. Because sentence against an evil deed is not executed speedily, the human heart is fully set to do evil. Though sinners do evil a hundred times and prolong their lives, yet I know that it will be well with those who fear God, because they stand in fear before him.

ECCLESIASTES 8:9-12

81

I n today's world, talk of "the economy" can hardly be separated from talk of "globalization." People are becoming more and more aware of the fact that the entire world is interconnected. Yet this realization seems to bring with it a kind of paralysis, a sense that it is impossible to influence or affect this development. Some sort of anonymous system, it seems, forces us to fall into line, leaving us powerless to do anything but stick to our daily routine. Nico Roozen, director of the Netherlands-based interchurch development organization Solidaridad, has described this as a world in which "superficial consideration of the possible, or colorless compromise, is elevated to the norm."[1]

The rise of globalization has seen technology eclipse economics as the driving force behind human progress. Technology is nothing new — recall the technical progress of those who wanted to make a name for themselves in Genesis 4. Yet in the nineteenth and twentieth centuries, technology has taken on a different character than ever before. Jacques Ellul draws a distinction between what he calls "technique" and "Technique."[2] The former refers to the way technology developed for centuries between the years 1000 and 1750. During this time, the world saw a continuous but slow pace of technical development, based on millions of experiments in every field — in small industry, in transportation, in economics. Society absorbed these changes easily, growing rather than suffering shock.[3]

Yet the violence of the market in the nineteenth century brought about a significant change: the rise of Technique, that is, not only the engine but also technological progress as a system. With the uprooting of the English countryside and similar developments elsewhere, Technique managed to flow beyond societal boundaries, drowning the individual, who was unprotected against the onslaughts of Technique and the state. The result of all this was that traditional structure and ingrained traditions were slowly but surely crushed. The inventor ruled. Industry, the middle class, and the state as one body strove to find the optimal technical means, in spite of many public demonstrations against the machine, such as those of the Luddites. Even Karl Marx joined in, proclaiming that technique with

1. Nico Roozen, "Address on the Occasion of the Start of the Utz Kapeh Coffee Initiative," The Hague, December 4, 2003.

2. Jacques Ellul, *The Technological System,* trans. Joachim Neugroschel (New York: Continuum, 1980).

3. Jacques Ellul, *The Technological Society,* trans. John Wilkinson (New York: Knopf, 1964).

its production powers in the framework of the "capitalist mode of production" would be of decisive historical importance, transforming the entire economic structure of society, in a way incomparable to any earlier age.[4] After the 1850s, when slowly Europe's prosperity began to trickle down to the laboring classes, the belief took hold that all of human existence would be changed through technical progress. Belief in progress became universal, embraced by right and left alike.

The difference between technique and Technique is not therefore one of quantity, but of quality, even though today there are so many more technological developments than in the past. What changed the former into the latter can be seen in today's almost complete lack of obstacles to technological development. Any new technique is judged by no other criterion than that of the Technique itself; it calculates its own efficiency. Standards of justice, ethics, theology, aesthetics, and so on — all must, in the end, out of pure necessity, succumb to the only optimum choice: "the sole most efficient solution, the least of all evils." Even economics, politics, psychology, and organizational science have become Technique, subject to what Ellul calls the Technical System or the "technicist phenomenon." The modern individual has, so to speak, become the raw material for this technical development — primarily an observer, and completely powerless. In his individual and social life he experiences everywhere the results of such an anonymous development, against which there is little defense and which must be accepted in order not to perish or be excluded.

Ellul draws a dramatic picture that encompasses all fields of culture. Only technique is called upon to counteract the harmful effects of Technique, which in turn reinforces the technicist system with its totalitarian tendencies. Such tendencies, it should be noted, are identical in the democratic and the dictatorial state. Consider the propaganda methods that

---

4. Technique, manifesting itself in numerous fields and specialties, is endless. All those special fields — ranging from agrarian, industrial, military, transport techniques to techniques of communication, propaganda, education, and economic, financial, accounting, legal technique, scientific technique, medical technique and space technique, etc. (a complete list is impossible) — gear into the Technical "system" and influence each other. The system behaves, as Ellul has observed, in an automatic way; it is self-growing; it is universal, autonomous, and indivisible. The market, under its tendency to annex the whole of societal life (including healthcare and other domains which by nature are noncommercial), is a technical-economic mechanism, a subsystem of Technique, which is supposed to be self-regulating in the same way.

dominate the American elections: how much of what is said has to do with real political content, and how much is merely the effect of monetary investment into the political campaign?

The web of progress is becoming ever more tangled, as so-called advances reveal their unforeseen side effects — modern warfare, for instance, is an effect of the technical society. And so we find ourselves in a "technical environment." The remedy? More Technique, of course. And so Technique reinforces Technique, just as the state reinforces the state. Even states that want to deregulate can do so only on the basis of their large technical influence. Medical care and education are less and less directed by their own built-in norms, and more and more by the formulae required by the technical society. Our society is no longer focused on goals but on means, governed as it is by instruments automatically produced by its own technology. Globalization is now just as inevitable as the emergence of the atom bomb. Traditional communities and cultural minorities are doomed. Freedom of choice and governing options have essentially disappeared, because the one and only solution is the technical one: it provides the means, it is the best way, and so there is no alternative.

Yet this feeling of powerlessness is also not new. The writers of the Bible knew it, and the book of Ecclesiastes in particular provides us with an eloquent example. The words of the Preacher, or the Collector, as the name of the book's writer may be translated, are in essence a reflection on his perceptions of what he has observed "under the sun," in the world of human experience. Refraining from speculating on what happens "above the sun," the book's constant refrain is, "This is what I have discovered in my wanderings on earth." The author's powerlessness and frustration can be traced to the power-brokers, to those who have climbed the ladder of success in the system, and whose influence in this world remains unchecked. The "bad apples" flourish but the righteous are persecuted. "One person exercises authority over another to the other's hurt" (Eccles. 8:9). This is the view of a merciless realist.

Blame poverty on oppression: oppression through power, through dictatorship, through slippery bureaucracies. This is the case everywhere today. This biblical observation is entirely up-to-date. Indeed, its criticism is so cogent that some translators soften it, make it more conventional, more palatable. Other translators, fortunately, offer strong criticism to the role of the king. Consider the following translations of Ecclesiastes 5:8:

But in all, a king is an advantage to a land with cultivated fields. (KJV)

But all things considered, this is an advantage for the land: a king for a plowed field. (NRSV)

The increase from the land is taken by all; the king himself profits from the fields. (NIV)

The profit of a land is in everything; a king is subject to land. (Jacques Ellul)

Thus the greatest advantage in all the land is his [the king's]: he controls a field that is cultivated. (JPS)

The shift in meaning here is apparent, and a look at the world around us confirms the accuracy of the latter set of translations. In many of the Latin American countries, as well as in Asia and especially Africa, the majority of the postcolonial governments do not promote small farm and market gardens. What they do control to a large extent are the economic resources for their own benefit. These form their power base; the state is regarded as their private domain, because these authoritarian rulers are completely dependent on the income of the state, on taxes and often especially on foreign — that is, globalized — assistance. On these financial sources is their authority based, not on democratic support in the civil society.

Thus Ecclesiastes confirms that we should not have false notions about power, foreshadowing Jesus' words that "the rulers of the Gentiles lord it over them, and their great ones are tyrants over them" (Matt. 20:25). The book's author issues a warning on the nature of power as it exploits the land. He continues, "The lover of money will not be satisfied with money; nor the lover of wealth with gain. This also is vanity" (Eccles. 5:10).

Ecclesiastes affirms the unfathomable mystery of life in this world: "Even love! Even hate! Man knows none of these in advance — none!" "Men's hearts are full of sadness, and their minds of madness, while they live." "A man cannot even know his time." Human beings are "as fishes enmeshed in a fatal net."[5] But in the face of all this, the book's author makes a

5. Eccles. 9:1, 3, 12 (JPS).

decision: this all may be true. . . . "Yet I know that it will be well with those who fear God, because they stand in fear before him" (Eccles. 8:12). How can this be? How can we believe that all will be well when the godless prosper while the righteous are forgotten? When the wicked live long and prosper while the righteous suffer?

Here is where Ecclesiastes' central idea of "vanity" comes in. This situation is fleeting, like a vapor. God has not designed the world this way: it is merely human beings who treat one another in this terrible way. "God will judge the righteous and the wicked, for he has appointed a time for every matter, and for every work" (Eccles. 3:17). Note that the text doesn't say, "If you fear God, you'll become happy." It especially does not mean this in the modern Western sense of happiness as comfort, material wealth, or success.[6] Indeed, the opposite may be the case. Ecclesiastes' message is that in the fear of God, happiness can be found. In spite of everything, I know that everything will "go well with me" (Deut. 5:33) when I fear God — *because* I fear God. This is not the conclusion of systematic theology, nor a scientific pronouncement. Ecclesiastes doesn't bother with pious platitudes or easy reassurances or conventional wisdom. Of all the things that fall under the category of vanity, only faith is the exception. Even wisdom is vanity. The Preacher *decides to choose the knowledge of faith.*

The very fear of God assures God's presence.[7] God does not rule the world, but he will do so. Thus we pray, "Your kingdom come." But God rules already wherever the fear of God can be found. He rules already for those who have received him. Through those who follow him, the kingdom is already in our midst.[8] In the Bible, "fear of the Lord" is an act of closer intimacy; it is not a paralyzing terror. It is nothing like worldly fear of the kind condemned by Jesus in the parable of the talents: "Master, I knew that you were a harsh man, reaping where you did not sow, and gathering where you did not scatter seed; so I was afraid, and I went and hid your talent in the ground. Here you have what is yours" (Matt. 25:24-25).

In Ecclesiastes and throughout the Bible, we see that faith can only be faith when it is lived in dialogue with our own lives and relates to all our questions. It can only grow when we confront the contradictions, disap-

6. Jacques Ellul, *Métamorphose du bourgeois* (Paris: Calmann-Lévy, 1967), pp. 67-108.

7. Jacques Ellul, *Reason for Being: A Meditation on Ecclesiastes,* trans. Joyce Main Hanks (Grand Rapids: Eerdmans, 1990).

8. René Girard, *Job, the Victim of His People,* trans. Yvonne Freccero (Stanford: Stanford University Press, 1987).

pointments, joys, and vanities of life. To believe means to acknowledge the "And yet. . . ."

And yet I choose nonconformity. And yet I refuse to abandon this knowledge. Based on that, the same God, whose works we can neither fathom nor discover (Eccles. 8:17), will certainly reveal himself as the unique shepherd (Eccles. 12:11).

CHAPTER 16

Exclusion

The word of the Lord came to me: Mortal, prophesy against the shepherds of Israel: prophesy, and say to them — to the shepherds: Thus says the Lord GOD: Ah, you shepherds of Israel who have been feeding yourselves! Should not shepherds feed the sheep? You eat the fat, you clothe yourselves with the wool, you slaughter the fatlings; but you do not feed the sheep. You have not strengthened the weak, you have not healed the sick, you have not bound up the injured, you have not brought back the strayed, you have not sought the lost, but with force and harshness you have ruled them. So they were scattered, because there was no shepherd; and scattered, they became food for all the wild animals. My sheep . . . were scattered over all the face of the earth, with no one to search or seek for them. . . .

As for you, my flock, thus says the Lord GOD: I shall judge between sheep and sheep, between rams and goats: is it not enough for you to feed on the good pasture, but you must tread down with your feet the rest of your pasture? When you drink of clear water, must you foul the rest with your feet? And must my sheep eat what you have trodden with your feet, and drink what you have fouled with your feet?

EZEKIEL 34:1-6, 17-19

In this chapter we are going to discuss different shepherds — shepherds who do not feed their sheep, but feed themselves (Ezek. 34:8). They are the rich landowners who have claimed the most fertile land. In the late

88

1970s I made a short camping trip from Buenos Aires to the Neuquén province in West Argentina. While in the Andes Mountains we encountered a small, isolated, and needy indigenous community. There were no men, only women and children, all suffering from various diseases. The men had left to earn meager pay as shepherds hundreds of kilometers away in the valley, where large property owners had occupied the best land since colonial times. These owners had driven out the original inhabitants, who had settled in ever higher and less hospitable regions. Because of the chilly climate and the snowfall, the villagers I encountered had a growing season of only three months. The apples remained small and green. Unripe fruit caused diarrhea and a high rate of infant mortality.

Economic oppression in today's world no longer has to do exclusively with exploitation in the form of forced labor or wages that are not high enough to allow workers to make a living. It also encompasses the multitudes of poor people who are simply excluded from the economic process. The current system simply has no need for indigenous people and other cultural minorities, with their "primitive," "backward" ways that do not center on the idea of profit. If the current system thinks of such persons at all, it thinks only that they should be grateful for the progress the rich have managed to make, for the rich then can provide them opportunities to develop themselves.

Yet the prophet Ezekiel pulls no punches when he addresses the self-righteousness of the rich. God says, "I'll teach them a lesson! I want my sheep back and I will destroy the meadows where your sheep graze." In today's terms, this might read, "I will put an end to these job-creating investments of theirs! The shepherds will no longer feed themselves." "I will rescue my sheep from their mouths, so that they may not be food for them" (Ezek. 34:10). The wealthy have taken possession of the world's economic resources, yet God addresses them as shepherds, in effect reminding them that they ought to be their brothers' keepers. God sees them as human beings, not as powerless officials in the Technical system of which they are a part. Of course, the kind of economic system we have today did not exist in Ezekiel's time, but there was still a great division between rich and poor. And Ezekiel's message is clearly addressed to "the nations" as well as to Israel (34:28-29).

The metaphor goes further. The rich and the violent are compared to the sheep themselves, as God proclaims that he will judge between the rams and the he-goats (Ezek. 34:22). "Is it not enough," he asks, "for you to feed on the good pasture, but you must tread down with your feet the rest of your pasture?" The elite in Latin America and the middle class in rich and becoming-rich nations are not always aware of the suffering their actions cause, thanks to a system in which everything becomes anonymous, in which the poor are out of sight.

In his book *The Embarrassment of Riches* (Knopf, 1987), historian Simon Schama describes the Golden Age of the Netherlands.[1] In that era, a culture of "abundance and discomfort" dominated: the rich merchants of Amsterdam did not flout their wealth publicly, but maintained a modest lifestyle and gave liberally to ecclesiastical funds for the needy. Contrast this with our times, wherein wealth is shamelessly displayed. At a 2000 campaign dinner, George W. Bush, soon to be the next president of the United States, welcomed his supporters as "the haves and the have-mores." His words were greeted with applause.

Of course, modern shamelessness about wealth goes hand-in-hand with the facelessness of the modern state, which devises its regulations and laws without any input from the common people. And once the technical preparation of the decision process has taken place, the matter is implemented, no matter what. I once attended a worship service in which a group of young people performed a play about the problem of poverty. One of its songs had the following refrain:

> In the land of the blind One-Eye is king,
> Officials with their crooked sight
> make money and profit their mainspring,
> ignoring human and nature's plight.

The powerless officials in a faceless system, with their "crooked sight," can do nothing else but rubber-stamp decisions about problems whose origins lie within that exact same system. Powerless to effect real change, they depend on technicians, planners, economic experts, managers of public health and education, and public relations experts to tell them what to do. These same experts are relied upon to revise the communication apparatus when some governmental decision meets with opposition in society — it is not a matter of changing the law; it is simply a matter of explaining the is-

---

1. Simon Schama, *The Embarrassment of Riches: An Interpretation of Dutch Culture in the Golden Age* (New York: Knopf, 1987).

sue more "efficiently." Issues are so formulated that they fit into a system wherein one functionary oversees the other (Eccles. 5:8). Numbers are decisive. Are there too many refugees or asylum-seekers in the country, according to the official tally? Then some have to go. Why? Because the optimum number has been calculated by the authorities. Thus the human element disappears and the criterion for managing becomes managing itself.

The poor in our Technique-dominated world are poor not only because they have little or no income; they are poor as well because they are excluded from the system. Classical notions of property and of the origins of the "poor classes" are no longer valid. The capital lacking in the Global South is mainly of a social nature: education, health care, infrastructure, and access to the services provided by public utilities. Also lacking, of course, are jobs and the right to obtain a pension. And lacking are the media that are so important in today's society and that could offer the poor a platform by which to have a voice in the public square; there are very few, if any, newspapers or television channels devoted to the poor.

The forgotten people of this earth do not only suffer from individual poverty; their destitution is collective and political as well. Famine and violence are almost taboo topics within the Technical community, even though they are widespread, and thereby give the lie to globalization, as Ellul points out. "The real poor," he says, "are the ethnical and cultural forgotten minorities, who have no single chance for independence, are on the point of being wiped out, and are always on the wrong side of the argument."[2]

Some may object, arguing that economic growth is necessary, that it depends on good entrepreneurial skills, which, in turn, are driven by the profit motive. After all, they say, entrepreneurship creates jobs and so combats poverty. That is true as far as it goes, but it fails to take into account the "exclusion mechanism" inherent in the Technical system. A prominent Peruvian economist, Adolfo Figueroa, has articulated a new theory of economic development that accounts for this mechanism for inclusion and exclusion within the all-powerful capitalistic system.[3] He points out the blind spot of current economic thinking, which assumes that the national communities and the global ones are, from a social, political, and cultural per-

2. Jacques Ellul, *The Betrayal of the West,* trans. Matthew J. O'Connell (New York: Seabury, 1978).

3. Adolfo Figueroa, *La Sociadad Sigma: una teoría del desarrollo económico* (Mexico/Lima: Fondo de Cultura Económica, 2003).

spective, all similar. But not all parts of society function according to the suppositions of Western capitalism. The current income disparity is caused by structural inequality, which, in turn, can be explained by social patterns that are historically different. In capitalism, he explains, there is the problem of an unequal beginning. The poor of the cultural minorities — who in many countries are the majority — are excluded from the economic process because they have not historically been able to invest the same "start-capital." They are in effect fighting a battle with unequal weapons. They cannot possibly prevail against the Technical system. They not only lack the physical or financial capital, but they especially are short on the cultural and political funds, and so cannot assert their rights. That's the reason why wealth does not trickle down and is the root cause why riches and poverty fail to converge, as economic theory teaches they should. For decades already the gulf between rich and poor, between modern and traditional sectors, has been becoming wider. That disparity is fundamental: it is cemented into the foundation of society itself. The capitalistic economic-political framework is hierarchical, and ethnic minorities are not part of this hierarchy but at most on the very lowest level possible.

Current theory blames the inequality on a lack of assertion on the part of the poor within the system; Figueroa shows that certain sections of society are not even included in the system. This creates underclasses in society, with no rights. Investments in such a fundamentally unequal society only create more disparity. This explains the failure of the development decades. The structural political and cultural imbalance is a given that simply remains outside the perspective of economic theory. The World Bank and the IMF simply don't see why a reformation of development is of the utmost necessity, writes Figueroa.

In his well-known book *Small Is Beautiful*, E. F. Schumacher writes, "The common criterion for success, namely, the growth of national income is utterly misleading and, in fact, must of necessity lead to phenomena which can only be described as neocolonialism."[4] This doesn't mean, of course, that the rich purposefully "push with flank and shoulder and butt at all the weak animals with horns until they scatter far and wide" (Ezek. 34:21), thereby excluding the poor from the economic process. In general, they don't mean to do this. We would do injustice to our entrepre-

4. E. F. Schumacher, *Small Is Beautiful: Economics as if People Mattered* (New York: Harper Perennial, 1989).

neurs to accuse them of actual intent to do this. But, continues Schumacher, this makes the problem larger instead of smaller. In the perverted Technicist system, discussed in the previous chapter, the course of events is also determined by the best intentions. "Methods of production, standards of consumption, criteria of success and failure, systems of values, and behavior patterns establish themselves in poor countries which, being (doubtfully) appropriate only to conditions of affluence already achieved, fix the poor countries ever more inescapably in a condition of utter dependence on the rich."[5]

The ultimate conclusion is that, just as Figueroa points out, we must be highly critical of economic theory as taught in our universities today. Science needs a connection to Truth. Says Psalm 119, "I have more understanding than all my teachers. . . . Through your precepts I get understanding; therefore I hate every false way" (vv. 99, 104). In that same psalm, the psalmist writes: "I have chosen the way of faithfulness. . . . Turn my heart to your decrees, and not to selfish gain" (vv. 30, 36). In that way we can see through the ideology, the aggressive marketing strategy, political propaganda, and television. Then we are aware that "in their greed they will exploit you with deceptive words" (2 Peter 2:3). The mass media of the Technical society are insufficient for us. We drink from our own wells.

5. Schumacher, *Small Is Beautiful.*

CHAPTER 17

The Matthew Effect

And he told them many things in parables, saying: "Listen! A sower went out to sow. And as he sowed, some seeds fell on the path, and the birds came and ate them up. Other seeds fell on rocky ground, where they did not have much soil, and they sprang up quickly, since they had no depth of soil. But when the sun rose, they were scorched; and since they had no root, they withered away. Other seeds fell among thorns, and the thorns grew up and choked them. Other seeds fell on good soil and brought forth grain, some a hundredfold, some sixty, some thirty. Let anyone with ears listen!"

Then the disciples came and asked him, "Why do you speak to them in parables?" He answered, "To you it has been given to know the secrets of the kingdom of heaven but to them it has not been given. For to those who have, more will be given, and they will have an abundance; but from those who have nothing, even what they have will be taken away."

MATTHEW 13:3-12

It should be clear by now that the economic derailment in the Third World cannot be simply offloaded on the shoulders of private enterprise. By and large the intentions of entrepreneurs and businessmen are honorable. They know their jobs; many of them do excellent work. It is also clear that they can do nothing without help from the state and from technology, which provide them with a network, a basis, and a work envi-

94

ronment. The historian Richard Tawney has remarked, "Few tricks of the unsophisticated intellect are more curious than the naïve psychology of the business man, who ascribes his achievements to his own unaided efforts, in blind unconsciousness of a social order without whose continuous support and vigilant protection he would be as a lamb bleating in the desert."[1] Tawney calls this "the complex of the individualist." Fortunately, in the decades since he wrote these words many entrepreneurs have acquired a new vision regarding the social order; not only do they realize that they depend on this order, but also they often strive to act in socially responsible ways.

The liberal notion that what my own labor earns can be attributed entirely to my own efforts and choices is not a recent one. Tawney cites a seventeenth-century Puritan pamphlet which reads, "No question, but riches should be the portion rather of the godly than of the wicked where it is good for them, for godliness hath promises of this life as well as of the life to come." Particularly in the United States there has been a tradition of sermons that promise that those who live pious lives will be rewarded with economic success, and this has often come to be equated with Christian economic thinking. Indeed, the Western model, both religious and nonreligious, of *Homo economicus* regards success as a matter of personal merit — my wealth is proof of my economic virtues. This image and mindset have their origin in the Western European middle class but are now applied to others as well: those who have no money, those who have failed to "amount to something," those who are poor, those who are misfits. This kind of self-justification, of course, is diametrically opposed to justification by faith.

Yet the pious capitalist thinks she knows the Bible. Doesn't Jesus himself say that those who have will receive more? When you don't have money you can't earn money. Money makes money; you have to invest. No pain, no gain. If you have only a little, you can lose that little quickly in the competitive marketplace. So take care! Exploit your talents with the sole aim of earning more; that's the only way, to go for more. Such lines of thought are all based on Matthew 13:12 or Matthew 25:29; indeed, the phenomenon they express has come to be known as the "Matthew effect" — that is, the rich get richer, while the poor get poorer.

The trouble, of course, is that Matthew-effect thinking transposes Je-

---

1. Richard Tawney, *Religion and the Rise of Capitalism: A Historical Study* (New York: Harcourt, Brace, 1937).

sus' words to our private economic lives, which is not the intention of this parable. Ellul notes that Technique attacks the heart. The technicist culture which has proven so successful that it has caused the human psyche itself to undergo a metamorphosis: the individual in modern society is no longer situated in relation to other people, but is fully oriented around Technique. "This complete mutation of the human species has not been produced by a collectivist theory or by someone's will to power," he writes. "The cause is much more profound, at once human and inhuman; inhuman because it is occasioned by things and circumstances, human because it answers the heart's desire of every modern man, without exception."[2] People with such hearts of iron cannot help but interpret the Bible accordingly. Yet no greater contradiction is possible than between the words of Jesus and the proclamation of those who see money in everything.

After Jesus tells the Parable of the Sower, the disciples question his use of parables. Jesus replies, "To you it has been given to know the secrets of the kingdom of heaven, but to them it has not been given." And then come these mysterious words: "For to those who have, more will be given, and they will have abundance; but from those who have nothing, even what they have will be taken away" (Matt. 13:12). Words like these appear throughout the Gospels when Jesus is asked to explain why he teaches in parables. They are often misunderstood, and because we do not properly understand them, we tend to give them the most banal application possible. The truth is that neither the Parable of the Sower nor the Parable of the Talents has anything at all to do with money.

What, then, do these enigmatic words mean? They want to express that God's word is not some sort of advertisement message. The Bible is neither a book of common-sense wisdom, nor of a "hidden," abstract theory. And it is most certainly not a book that employs the means of modern communication strategy, wherein a "sender" conveys a "message" to a "recipient" in order to influence him. Modern advertising relies on simple, clear, aggressive messages for its effectiveness. Jesus' message isn't designed to fit on a billboard or in a 30-second television commercial. It is not available in sound bites; it is not a collection of freestanding doctrines from which we can pick and choose when we want to. This is why Jesus uses parables rather than sermons in public.

2. Jacques Ellul, *The Technological Society,* trans. John Wilkinson (New York: Knopf, 1964).

Jesus doesn't regard his hearers as mere passive receivers of a message, as modern communication theory would have it. For among these multitudes there are those who cannot possibly comprehend the secret, while there are others who are already part of it, who share in that mystery. After all, the Spirit is present both in the act of speaking and that of listening. A sermon by itself cannot guarantee understanding. The recipient participates in the sermon! The speaker and the listener belong to the same communion of saints: both grasp the direction of Jesus' words. Even Jesus does not speak for himself. Both speaker and listener are dependent on the great Third party: the communion with the Spirit which is behind the words and the understanding of them. Both speaker and listener are embraced by this mystery. The intended target is those who both have ears to hear and eyes to see. About the understanding listener, the Dutch hymnodist Jan Wit comments that he is "surrounded by the mystery, expelled by everything, but all things matter to him." A contemporary artist said it thus, "You can't discuss a mystery: it can only grab a person."

Karen Armstrong tells that Baba Metsia, one of the rabbis in Jesus' time, remarked, "God does not come to man oppressively, but commensurately with a man's power of receiving him."[3] People hear it, but they don't grasp it. "But blessed are your eyes for they see, and your ears, for they hear. Truly I tell you, many prophets and righteous people longed to see what you see, but did not see it, and to hear what you hear and did not hear it" (Matt. 13:16-17). But it has been "revealed" to infants (Matt. 11:25). In other words, the message is for those particular hearers whose minds are already open to the mystery, who already are included. "The measure you give will be the measure you get" (Mark 4:24). It's the listeners who are at stake. It's a matter of involvement; if they are participants, if they have already shared, then they will grow: they will be given even more and they will receive in abundance; but from those who have nothing, even what they have will be taken away.

This is why in Mark 4:24 Jesus says, "Pay attention to what you hear," "Consider carefully" what you hear, which also means how you hear and why you hear. While listening to Jesus' words, we are no passive consumers. We are no disinterested onlookers. We are no critics of his sermon. Of course, we can keep him at a distance; we can report on him as an interest-

3. Karen Armstrong, *A History of God: The 4000-Year Quest of Judaism, Christianity, and Islam* (New York: Gramercy, 2004).

ing phenomenon. We can listen with an ear to self-affirmation or, perhaps, consider him an attack on our existence. We may already have a rebuttal ready or even try to trip him up on something, or subject his words to a rational analysis. If so, then we are like the Pharisees and the scribes who also listened, but their aim was to debate.

If that is the case, then the message is kept at a safe distance. One of the commentaries on these texts states that in Jesus' parables there are a thousand possibilities to circumvent the Messiah mystery. But to those who fathom the teaching — and that can be a matter of life-long learning — the hearing becomes heeding, cognition becomes recognition, a mystery turns into intimacy. The presence of the Messiah is a mystery that totally engulfs us, but we need not be secretive in talking about it. We are invited to be a parable ourselves, to compare ourselves with Jesus. A parable is typified by clear images, taken from everyday life. Paul would call these "readable letters" (2 Cor. 3:2-3). After all, "No one after lighting a lamp hides it under a jar, or puts it under a bed, but puts it on a lampstand, so that those who enter see the light. . . . Then pay attention to how you listen!" (Luke 8:16, 18).

CHAPTER 18

The Parable of the Talents

For [the kingdom of heaven] is as if a man going on a journey, summoned his slaves and entrusted his property to them; to one he gave five talents, to another two, to another one, to each according to his ability. Then he went away. The one who had received the five talents went off at once and traded with them, and made five more talents. In the same way, the one who had the two talents made two more talents. But the one who had received the one talent went off and dug a hole in the ground and hid his master's money. After a long time the master of those slaves came and settled accounts with them. Then the one who had received the five talents came forward, bringing five more talents, saying, "Master, you handed over to me five talents; see I have made five more talents." His master said to him, "Well done, good and trustworthy slave; you have been trustworthy in a few things, I will put you in charge of many things; enter into the joy of your master."

MATTHEW 25:14-21

Who among you would say to your slave who has just come in from plowing or tending sheep in the field, "Come here at once and take your place at the table"? Would you not rather say to him, "Prepare supper for me, put on your apron and serve me while I eat and drink; later you may eat and drink"? Do you thank the slave for doing what was commanded? So you also, when you have done all that you were ordered to do, say, "We are worthless slaves; we have done only what we ought to have done!"

W ell, there you have it! Here is proof that those who have money will receive more. After all, this parable plainly deals with money, right? It's about a slave who invests five talents and earns another five — a full hundred-percent gain — and his master praises him to high heaven! How could Jesus be any clearer? You put your money to work, or your talents and capabilities, and so fulfill your holy duty to expand.

But watch how you hear! Jesus speaks in parables, and a hallmark of parables is the use of common images that relate to people's everyday experiences. In the agrarian economy in which his listeners lived, everyone was familiar with seeding, with working the land, with lamps placed on lampstands, and so on. Yet we cannot take the images as embodying the essence of the message. When Jesus tells a parable about a lampstand, he does not mean to send his listeners off to the market to buy a particular kind of lampstand. Nor does he advise us here to invest our money to maximize its return. The successful investor in the parable is nothing more and nothing less than a symbol.

Jesus' parables are concerned with the kingdom of heaven and his listeners' relationship to that kingdom. Faith proclamation is different from moralizing. The Parable of the Talents is followed by that of the wise and foolish maidens who had to keep their lamps burning as they waited for the arrival of the bridegroom; in it, Jesus says, "Keep awake therefore; for you know neither the day nor the hour" (Matt. 25:1-13). And just before the Parable of the Talents, he says, "But about that day and hour no one knows, neither the angels in heaven, nor the Son" (Matt. 24:36). This hardly describes a reality in which an investor can take rational actions to reap benefits from his calculated risk.

Another, only seemingly similar, version of this parable can be found in Luke 19:11-27, where it is known as the Parable of the Pounds. The Lukan version has a totally different context. Jesus tells it to his disciples as they travel to Jerusalem. On this journey he has told them of how he must suffer, yet they have not understood him (Luke 18:34). Also on this journey Jesus has healed a blind person and has met the tax collector Zacchaeus, who, as a result of his meeting with Jesus, has promised to repay fourfold all the money he has obtained by fraud (Luke 19:8). This quadruple repayment could certainly not have been financed from the extortion itself, for that would only have resulted in a 100 percent repayment. The compensation must have come from the investment yields on his capital. The disciples are very impressed with Zacchaeus' conversion, especially in view of the fact that Jesus is so close now to Jerusalem, where, they believe, the kingdom of God will be revealed.

It is at this point that Luke records Jesus telling the Parable of the Pounds, and in context it is a downer. It's bad news because it goes against what is expected; it seems to go directly against the logic of the kingdom. This parable rests on a crisis. Jesus says, in effect, "Look around and describe what you see." And then he tells a tale that's as close to life as what we find in Ecclesiastes (see Chapter 15). He shows his disciples how secular power works. And like all parables, it connects to the everyday experiences of the time. It is entirely possible, indeed, that Jesus was referring specifically to Archelaus, King Herod's son. Herod was king of Judea when Jesus was born; when he died, Archelaus considered himself next in line to the throne. He set off to Rome to obtain official approval to become the next king of Judea. Yet at the same time, a delegation of fifty Judean men also made the trip to Rome specifically to oppose the appointment. Archelaus even at that time had a reputation for cruelty, and few Judeans wanted him for their king. Yet Archelaus received the appointment, and on his return he unsurprisingly took bloody revenge on the Jews: "But as for these enemies of mine who did not want me to be king over them — bring them here and slaughter them in my presence" (Luke 19:27). This master is a real despot.

The master in Luke's parable is therefore not the same master as in Matthew's. Matthew's concern is not the logic of earthly kingdoms, but the heavenly one. (This despite the fact that some scholars, including Joachim Jeremias, detect some carelessness in the way the story has been recorded or composed by Matthew.) Its intention is to indicate the Parousia, the appearance of the kingdom of heaven. The master in Matthew's parable goes abroad and hands his entire property over, dividing it among all his servants: it now belongs to them; they themselves are now the judges of what is right. The master has entered into a partnership with them, a beneficial relationship, a covenant; he has made himself vulnerable. They now live in the expectation of his return, yet there is no specified date for that return — hence the temptation to behave as though he is gone for good (Matt.

25:48-50). And when he unexpectedly returns, the master and servants together give account of their actions. They appraise their mutual enterprise
as equal partners. The master and the servants are in complete accord.

Contrast all this with Luke's parable. The master there summons
"some" of his slaves, gives ten pounds of money to this group of ten, and
tells them to trade with it so that, on his return, he will have benefited financially from their work. In this parable there is clearly an association
with money. Money breeds money: "Your pound has made ten pounds of
profit." Or five, or one, as the case may be: all are supposed to have equal
opportunity, as their starting capital amounts to one single pound. And
the profit-generators are rewarded with authority over ten and five cities,
with a high office in the power structure. The person who was unable to do
anything with that one pound has it taken from him; it will accrue to the
one who has become the most prosperous. That's how loyalty to worldly
rulers — and to money — is rewarded. Loyalty pays; disloyalty, or even a
degree of passivity, means disgrace. Somebody else benefits.

In the Parable of the Talents in Matthew the yield equals the amount
originally given. Matthew does not want to emphasize those elements of
the story that point to the good intentions of the servants; that is not
where the parable's center of gravity lies. Rather, the center is the talents.
The talents in themselves carry the multiplying power. This is how it is
with God's mercy. Matthew offers an uplifting message by which the
reader is not discouraged or left with a feeling of helplessness with respect
to how to solve the problem of her relationship to her master. It has nothing to do with being positive about one's faith. The talents by themselves
accomplish this, according to God's mercifulness.

Of course, in the kingdom as related in Matthew there is also a servant who makes no profit at all. For him the judgment is severe. The master tells him, in effect, "You have made a caricature of me and have
blamed me. In your eyes I am a person who has harvested where he has
not planted." This amounts to the great refusal of grace; it is the religion
of the heart turned to iron. Theologian Tom Naastepad says that the pious but sterile Christian congregation is one place where this kind of
mindset may be found. In the end, of course, money does enter the picture, for Jesus says, "The least you could have done was go to the bank and
deposit it there, from which I, as you yourself have said, could have
claimed it back with interest!" Yet this servant has not even wrapped his
talent in a cloth, as Luke's servant did with his pound. Rather, he buries it.

He leaves, abandons his ministry, burying it as one would bury a corpse. "In his hand is the living gift dead," says Naastepad. "Given to him, the talent suddenly turns into . . . money!"[1]

In his book *Eight Parables in Matthew and Luke*, Naastepad explores the symbolic significance of the numbers five, two, and one. There are five books of Moses — the Torah. Two signifies the continuing tradition of Moses and the Prophets. One is "the One Lord who reveals himself as the Living Torah, the law and the prophets in the unavoidable figure who is Christ." It is this Christ who is rejected by this servant. To the person who receives the one talent, this gift is "a foreign matter in his life; it doesn't form part of his existence. God's grace is something he can do without, and actually he prefers it that way." He is alienated from life. He is scared. He arranges matters in such a way that they don't touch him.

This kind of fear is highly offensive; it is nothing like the fear of the Lord, which is active, setting out on a journey, "drawing near" (Eccles. 5:1), an engaging into relationship. Fear of the Lord is not fright and not dread. It is reverence, awe. It is not familiarity; it is trust. At first there is the Word, God's approach to us; then follows the hearing, our reverence, us coming closer. "He who received the five talents came forward and brought him five more talents." The text says "received," not "had received," in the past perfect tense, as in Matthew 25:24 concerning the man who buried that one talent. He too comes forward, but it is not an advance in order to hear.

This text has to do with expectations. In the modern economy, we calculate "utility." But Christians live in the expectation of something different (Matt. 24:44). This sense of expectation, of dwelling within and out of expectation, comes directly from Jewish tradition. This is why Paul ends his theology about Israel (Rom. 9–12:3) with an exhortation, "I appeal to you therefore, brothers and sisters, by the mercies of God, to present your bodies as a living sacrifice, holy and acceptable to God" (12:1). Your bodies — Paul was a Jewish Bible reader! Not your ideas, but your physical, concrete earthly lives. That, says Paul, is your self-evident service — in a word, your ministry. Here, too, the image of slaves is used. And here the word "latreia" appears, a word which originally had the meaning of earning a wage or serving as a slave. This ministry does proclaim something. It's an activity that radiates, that tells its own tale.

---

1. Th. J. M. Naastepad, *Acht gelijkenissen uit Mattheus en Lukas* (Kampen: Kok, second printing, n.d.).

Luke 17:9 raises the question whether a slave ought to be thanked for his services. Jesus suggests not: we ought to do everything that we are ordered to do, he says, and after we have done all that, we must acknowledge that we, according to God's plan, have been "useless slaves." We did do what we were told, but only because we had to do it. We do not replace the work of the Messiah. We did not establish the kingdom. We did not employ "means" to obtain "goals." We did what we did because we had to do it. That doesn't mean that we say in advance, "It's a waste; it makes no sense; what's the use?" Only in retrospect must we admit that when we have done everything, we are "worthless." God is God. He has compassion on whom he has compassion (Rom. 9:15), regardless of our labors and regardless of the display of usefulness presented in our policy documents.

The futility — most English translations of Ecclesiastes use the word "vanity" — of our works is no excuse for passivity (because we have to do what we have to do), but it is, in retrospect, a confession. What do we confess? We confess the belief in the coming of the Messiah, the One who will accomplish it, the One whom we expect, no matter how engaged we are in his service. We are like the clay of the potter (Rom. 9:20-21); we are the raw material, in itself useless for creativity except for the design of the artist.

Conformity to the world (Rom. 12:2) implies that "we are ruled by the pursuit of utility and efficiency," says Jacques Ellul. This is the opposite of a life out of God's free grace, out of what Paul calls the understanding of God's will. And our good works? Useless, says Ellul, if they concern the coming of the Messiah. "This is no longer our concern. It is no longer in our hands." And that is most fortunate! What a relief! To help the world's poor? It is God's command, yet a useless exercise. Prayer? "Your heavenly Father knows that you need all these things" (Matt. 6:32). What's the use of preaching? It's God's command and yet it is useless service.

But if we think of ourselves as useless servants (Luke 17:10), quoting Ellul again,

> it is not God or Jesus who passes the verdict of inutility. It is we ourselves who must pronounce it on our work: "We are unprofitable servants." God does not judge us thus. He does not reject either us or our works. Or rather, he does not echo the verdict if we have passed it on ourselves. If (as Christ demands) we judge ourselves in

104

this way when we have done all we could do and accepted all our responsibility, if we are able to view our works and most enthusiastic enterprises with the distance and detachment and humor that enable us to pronounce them useless, then we may be assured of hearing God say: "Well done, good and faithful servant" (Matt. 25:21).[2]

2. Jacques Ellul, *The Politics of God and the Politics of Man,* trans. Geoffrey W. Bromiley (Grand Rapids: Eerdmans, 1972).

CHAPTER 19

Righteousness Exalts a Nation

"Why do we fast but you do not see? Why humble ourselves, but you do not notice?" Look, you serve your own interest on your fast day, and oppress all your workers. Look, you fast only to quarrel and to fight and to strike with a wicked fist. Such fasting as you do today will not make your voice heard on high. Is such the fast that I choose, a day to humble oneself? Is it to bow down the head like a bulrush, and to lie in sackcloth and ashes? Will you call this a fast, a day acceptable to the LORD?

Is not this the fast that I choose: to loose the bonds of injustice, to undo the thongs of the yoke. . . ? Is it not to share the bread with the hungry, and bring the homeless poor into your house; when you see the naked, to cover them, and not to hide yourself from your own kin? Then your light shall break forth like the dawn, and your healing shall spring up quickly; your vindication shall go before you, the glory of the LORD shall be your rear guard. Then you shall call, and the LORD will answer; you shall cry for help, and he will say, Here I am.

If you remove the yoke from among you, the pointing of the finger, the speaking of evil, if you offer your food to the hungry and satisfy the need of the afflicted, then your light shall rise in the darkness and your gloom be like the noonday. The LORD will guide you continually, and satisfy your needs in parched places, and make your bones strong; and you shall be like a watered garden, like a spring of water, whose waters never fail. Your ancient ruins shall be rebuilt;

you shall raise up the foundations of many generations; you shall be
called the repairer of the breach, the restorer of streets to live in.

ISAIAH 58:3-12

I n the last four chapters of the book, we have been considering matters
of personal troth and our own stance before God and human beings.
But our responsibility goes beyond that: we must, at the same time, be
concerned with the way society functions. For it is in society that the economic question and the political problem are equally of the utmost importance. In the last chapter we saw the reemergence of the city, whose importance we discussed earlier in the book, as the reward for those who
were in league with the authoritarian master in Luke 19. And in Chapter 15
we noticed how widespread is the tendency to claim personal power over
something that is really in the public domain.

This passage from Isaiah points toward something different: not the
exploitation of the city, but its rebuilding. Consider the conversion story of
the Dominican Bartolomé de las Casas. He had sailed with Columbus on
his second expedition to the New World in the year 1502, while only seven-
teen years old, serving as both soldier and priest. In the next twelve years
he also became an *encomendero,* a proprietor of lands and of the native
people living there. In the year 1514 he had his "Damascus road experience." While preparing his Pentecost sermon on the island of Trinidad, he
read in the apocryphal Book of Sirach the following: "If a person sacrifices
goods obtained illegally, then that offering is tainted and the gifts, obtained contrary to the law, are not acceptable" (34:18). They cannot be considered pleasing to the Lord.

The many Latin American dictators come to mind as well, along with
others, past and present, who cruelly suppress their people. Such rulers may
sometimes play the part of ostentatious benefactors, "donating" a school
building here, a public park there, a water filtration plant elsewhere, all to
curry favor with voters for political gain. Las Casas realized that building
churches in the colonies and financing religion with funds extorted from
the natives were in truth an abomination to the Lord. As Sirach points out,
"The bread of the needy is the life of the poor. Whoever deprives them of it
is a man of blood. To take away a neighbor's living is to murder him; to deprive an employee of his wages is to shed blood" (34:20-22).

Here was Las Casas's first conversion, from colonist to preacher. Following this conversion, he gave away his possessions. However, a second conversion was to take place twenty-five years later, and this time he would change from preacher to politician. For the rest of his long life after this second experience he forcefully advocated through juridical means the rights of the native population. Personal ethics alone cannot accomplish this, even though the process begins with them: "oppression makes the wise foolish" (Eccles. 7:7).

Political labor of that kind became for Las Casas a high calling. Of course, in his case and ours, it's not merely a question of obedience to the laws. There are many politicians whose rule of life is to conduct themselves according to the law. But this in itself is not enough. What matters is the content of the law, which may be wicked. Personal conduct is all-important; each human person is responsible, even if her actions do not contravene the law. In his commentary on the New Testament, John Calvin writes, "Those who want to cover their misdeeds with the law in essence double their wrongdoings." Likewise Abraham Kuyper, in a speech given at the Free University of Amsterdam in 1892, made mention of "the continuous violating of human rights globally, violation not only by the individual but also by means of the law and through the judges." To persist in righteous living — as we saw in the previous chapter in Matthew 24:48-50 — can only be accomplished in the expectation which Kuyper called "the belief in the last judgment, where your own consciousness of justice resides in the ordinances of your God."

This faith of the "last days," this eschatological vision, helps us to see matters in their true perspective. We don't have to "change the system" before we can start to improve society. To think in terms of "capitalism versus socialism" — a style of thinking that was prevalent until recently — has caused both frustration and paralysis. This way of protest, often called "prophetic" by the churches engaging in it, has often been nonproductive. The promoters of radical change, who in one scoop want to completely overturn the system — with the originators of the revolution retaining control, of course — have historically caused oceans of blood. We cannot and need not reverse the course of the entire world. No system can be regarded as unequivocally definite.

Take the problem of poverty. Sweeping statements accomplish nothing. Brazilian theologian Jung Mo Sung has remarked that the proponents of liberation theology, by condemning the market system as idolatrous and totalitarian, have forgotten that over against the institute of the market stands not the kingdom of God, but the eschatological belief in the coming of that kingdom. The faith in its ultimate arrival ought to provide room for alternatives and to create better rules of the game, a greater satisfaction of needs and a more human society. Such a faith in the coming of the kingdom will prevent us from overestimating the merits of any institution. In real life, any institution can only be replaced by a better one. For example, a poorly working market can be changed into one that functions better, and fair trade practices can replace unfair ones. In Chapter 21 this theme will receive more attention.

Isaiah 58 is an important text in Jewish life, taking a central place in the liturgy of the Day of Atonement, Yom Kippur. We read there that God's presence does not come without strings attached, cannot be separated from the pursuit of justice. This prophecy contains four deeply loaded sections.

First, Isaiah, in this passage, allies himself beyond any doubt with the disadvantaged, the vulnerable. He quite ironically relays the complaints of the pious people, the faithful churchgoers: "Why do we fast, but God does not see? Why humble ourselves, but he does not notice?" To this self-pitying cry the prophet poses his initial reply: the Lord's presence for which you are looking within your institutional religion is incompatible with the continuation of your economic practices. On your days of fasting you pursue your own interests and chase after your debtors. You keep on doing business and force your laborers to work harder. Your fasts result in quarrels and strife, and only serve to "strike with a wicked fist." The way you fast will not make your voice heard on high. Is this the sort of fast that I choose, a day for humans to starve? Can you call this a fast, a day pleasing to the Lord?

Second, after this comes an example of biblical "civil education." The prophetic text says, "Is not this the fast that I choose: to loose the bonds of injustice, to undo the thongs of the yoke, to let the oppressed go free, and to break every yoke?" That is the call to social justice, to worthwhile economic development and society building. Writes Levinas, "It transforms society precisely into that which makes it society." We saw this in our earlier discussion of the economics of honor, where Jesus in Matthew 15 quotes the prophet Isaiah, "these people honor me with their lips . . . and their worship of me is a human commandment learned by rote" (Isa. 29:13). Ayaan Hirsi Ali, when questioned in regard to her film *Submission* whether the projecting of Koran texts on the female body should be regarded as offensive, answered, "People who defend the religious text claim this, but in reality we ought to accuse religious teachings themselves, when they suppress women." That remark is in line with Matthew and Isaiah, about "teaching human precepts and doctrines."

Third, as Bible readers we may not treat the problem of social justice in the abstract, thinking that as long as we are ourselves politically correct and aligned ideologically with the right sort of thinking that our obligation to society has thereby been fulfilled. Just to condemn the oppression of capitalism and make a theoretical or ideological choice for an alternative societal system is not sufficient. Neither can we wash our hands by claiming to have voted for a more enlightened political party. Nor can we escape into bureaucratic solutions while refraining from actually doing anything through cleverly maneuvering away from self-involvement and co-responsibility. In this way little remains of our biblical calling. Indeed, this sort of inaction can result in renewed oppression.

That's why the prophets also say that obedience to God's Word is impossible without being personally involved with the neighbor, the other person encountered in the economy. "Share your bread with the hungry, welcome those unfortunate who have no home to go to. Clothe the naked." Those matters we cannot leave to "the system." Do not hide yourself from your own fellow citizens who are "your own kin" (v. 7). We can never combat an oppressive regime if we do not combat it in our daily practice. Why did Apartheid last so long in South Africa? Because the official policy went hand in hand with the unofficial sort, which manifested itself in a lack of respect for black people in everyday life and a failure to treat as equals those with whom white South Africans daily rubbed shoulders.

Fourth, there is the question of how such an example of justice-filled economics relates to our faith-life. What is the connection to our own inner life with God? All this becomes clear when we read the concluding part of this passage. When we care for our neighbor, when our primary aim is to choose his or her interests, especially in economic matters, this leads to repairing our connection to God, which we have severed by separating our service to him from our service to the neighbor (see Chapter 8). To act economically according to the Word of God, proclaims Isaiah, means to act justly toward the poor, as a simple token of faith obedience. It's not merely a matter of norms and values, of a praiseworthy ethic, often typified by being abstract, but an instance of faith in God's Word.

When we offer to the hungry that which we desire ourselves and satisfy the needs of the afflicted, then, says the prophet, our light shall rise in the darkness and our gloom be like the noonday. All this is part and parcel of redemption, of one's own salvation, of God reconstituting his fidelity in one's personal life. In this way our own needs are satisfied, our own wounds healed. The Jewish philosopher Levinas, commenting on this text, says that this is a change in the very basis of our being.

Your truthfulness will precede you. Your sense of justice will herald your approach. The Lord is your rear guard, where his glory illumines you, and so, from behind, provides protection for the voyage ahead. This ensures that God is no longer absent, as was the case in verse 4, in which our voice was not heard on high. We are the ones who make sure that he is in our midst. God comes behind us. Levinas boldly states that "we codetermine the existence of God." When we pursue his ways, God will back us up all the way. We can always rely on his protecting presence. He will follow. But he will be there too when we pray to him: when we call for help, he will answer, "Here I am." Says one hymn, "For a heart that's closed, Heaven's door is shut," quoting 1 John 4:8. But when that same heart opens itself up to see the plight of the oppressed and hungry, "when you don't hide yourself from your own kin," as Isaiah 58:7 has it, then "the LORD will guide you continually, and satisfy your needs in parched places, and make your bones strong; and you shall be like a watered garden, like a spring of water, whose waters never fail" (v. 11).

In other words, you will be blessed and be a blessing.

Blessed as a well-watered garden; and a blessing like a spring whose waters never fail. All this affects others too: that's the way to attract co-workers. Because, according to verse 12, as the Jewish translation has it, "Men from your midst shall rebuild ancient ruins, you shall restore foundations laid long ago." "Your own people will do the rebuilding," as another translation reads. We can remake society and the economy when we really set our mind to it, make it again a place where we can thrive. "Righteousness exalts a nation" (Prov. 14:34).

Yes, this concerns us personally. Ellul, in his commentary on the book of Jonah, writes,

> The word of God is not directed to humanity in general. It always is addressed to a particular person, from a specific nation, that very man or woman. Jonah is a good example. He is chosen to do something he alone can do. When God chooses a person then this hap-

111

pens because he or she will be of service in God's undertaking. He or she alone has that task, for which God has particularly equipped them to do so. God's choice in the election of that one person is not simply the announcement of the election, of being set apart, with our personal security as goal, or to the greater joy or higher edification of our own soul, so that we can have peace with the outcome. No, the Scriptures never mention such a matter as pure mystical calling. To be chosen by God is not a matter of knowing the general will of God but consists of being involved in concrete action, in a certain enterprise.

To be a Christian is not a simple case of only oneself being saved by Christ; God wants to use that person for the salvation of others through Christ. . . . When Jonah receives his call, when he actually becomes a saved person, it's for the sake of others. From the moment faith develops in us, the conviction must grow that the grace granted to us, is, in the first place, needed so that others can benefit. It never is a matter of pure personal satisfaction. Our salvation, our faith journey, this adventure of ours, is part of the salvation and adventure of those who surround us, and, eventually, of the world.[1]

1. Jacques Ellul, *The Judgment of Jonah*, trans. Geoffrey Bromiley (Grand Rapids: Eerdmans, 1971).

CHAPTER 20

Society and Community

A capable wife who can find? She is far more precious than jewels. . . . She seeks wool and flax, and works with willing hands. She is like the ships of the merchant, she brings her food from far away. She rises while it is still night and provides food for her household and tasks for her servant girls. She considers a field and buys it; with the fruit of her hands she plants a vineyard. She girds herself with strength, and makes her arms strong. She perceives that her merchandise is profitable. Her lamp does not go out at night. She puts her hands to the distaff, and her hands hold the spindle. She opens her hands to the poor and reaches out her hands to the needy.

PROVERBS 31:10, 13-20

My brothers and sisters, do you with your acts of favoritism really believe in our glorious Lord Jesus Christ? For if a person with gold rings and in fine clothes comes into your assembly, and if a poor person in dirty clothes also comes in, and if you take notice of the one wearing the fine clothes and say, "Have a seat here, please," while to the one who is poor you say, "Stand there," or, "Sit at my feet," have you not made distinctions among yourselves, and become judges with evil thoughts? Listen, my beloved brothers and sisters. Has not God chosen the poor in the world to be rich in faith and to be heirs of the kingdom that he has promised to those who love him?

JAMES 2:1-5

A capable wife: her value exceeds that of jewels. Seemingly this text is all about the woman as an object of economic value. However, we can excuse the writer of Proverbs from having a vision of the female partner as economic property; he (or possibly she) permits the use of poetic symbolism: after all, nothing has greater value than a capable woman as wife — "and let her works praise her in the city gates" (v. 31).

In all preceding chapters that touched upon economic references within the Bible one thing stands out: nowhere does the Bible deal with economics in the modern sense of the word. The Bible has no quarrel with economics as such. However, when it does touch on economic matters, it is always within the context of practicing justice. Economics is simply part of everyday life as experienced in agriculture, animal husbandry, commerce, city-building, wage labor, the use of slaves, monetary matters where the prohibition of charging interest features prominently, rights of redemption (Lev. 25:23-34; Ruth 4), general duties to financially maintain the priestly class (Lev. 6:16, 7:6, 24:9), as well as taxes. All these touch on the day-to-day conditions of living, with justice as the focal point: honest balance, honest weights (Lev. 19:36), which means an honest price. "Treasures gained by wickedness do not profit, but righteousness delivers from death" (Prov. 10:2). "Surely oppression makes the wise foolish, and a bribe corrupts the heart" (Eccles. 7:7). These passages all directly point to honesty and sincere regard for the economic welfare of the other. The Torah, the prophets, the wisdom literature, all look at the economy from a justice point of view. The rich who have acquired their wealth at the expense of their work force are sharply condemned (see Chapter 16): "Listen. The wages of the laborers who mowed your fields, which you kept back by fraud, cry out. . . . You have condemned and murdered the righteous one, who does not resist you" (James 5:4-6).

The New Testament is in full agreement with the Old Testament in this regard. Righteousness is religion: "Beware of practicing your piety before others in order to be seen by them; for then you have no reward from your Father in heaven. So whenever you give alms, do not sound a trumpet before you, as the hypocrites do in the synagogues and in the streets, so that they may be praised by others" (Matt. 6:1-3). "The righteous live by their faith" (Hab. 2:4; Rom. 1:17; Gal. 3:11; Heb. 10:38). Rabbi Ignaz Maybaum has written, "The freedom which creates man's political, economic and cultural life is derived from the freedom of worship."[1]

---

1. Ignaz Maybaum, *The Face of God after Auschwitz* (Amsterdam: Polak & Van Gennep, 1965).

The modern world's economic problems were nonexistent in biblical times: no such things existed as dishonesty in global world trade or unstable global markets or economic crises such as the permanent burden of third world debt: our situation is simply different. Crises in the economy then did not originate in the economy itself, as is the case today, but were a direct result of natural disasters, droughts, locust plagues, or wartime destruction. When the Bible mentioned production, the wisdom literature simply pointed to the importance of work, because "the way of the sluggard is overgrown with thorns," or, as Proverbs 24:33-34 has it, "A little sleep, a little slumber . . . , and poverty will come upon you like a robber."

What we now call the "war on poverty" was then an unknown factor, was simply not the burning question it now is in modern world society. The fact that there were rich and poor was taken for granted. The real issue was mutual respect. Proverbs 22:2 reminds us, "The rich and the poor have this in common: the LORD is the maker of them all." The Bible continuously makes statements such as this one in Deuteronomy 14:29 that "the resident aliens, the orphans, and the widows in your towns, may come and eat their fill." Those are words that impress upon the reader the plight of the poor. "If you take your neighbor's cloak in pawn, you shall restore it before the sun goes down; for it may be your neighbor's only clothing to use as a cover; in what else shall that person sleep?" (Exod. 22:26-27). We have to place ourselves in our neighbor's shoes, because life is not an abstraction: we deal with people of flesh and blood. Fortunately there are people within and outside the church who are concerned about asylum seekers, persons often reduced to anonymous, indistinct objects in the eyes of indifferent government officials.

The pre-capitalistic economy was embedded into a society that was composed of personal economic relationships. The economy did not yet dominate society but was a part of it. Writes the Dutch anthropologist Henk Tieleman, referring to the interaction between economy and culture, "The function of barter was not commerce, but the consolidation of good relations."[2] By no stretch of imagination had the economy then reverted to Technique, or become a self-regulating and anonymous system.

So how did things change with the rise of capitalism, in which the church had to position itself? Tawney observes that the clergy failed to bring

---

2. Henk Tieleman, *In het teken van de economie. Over de wisselwerking van economie en cultuur* (Baarn: Ambo, 1991).

a message relevant to the emerging modern society, ignoring the developments in the monetary system and international trade, and therefore unable to understand their implications. In their sermons the clergy simply repeated the traditional understandings of Bible texts dealing with the traditional economy, and, failing to analyze modern developments, were unable to move forward. Tawney writes that the church "had tried to moralize economic relations, by treating every transaction as a case of personal conduct, involving personal responsibility. In an age of impersonal finance, world-markets, and a capitalist organization of industry, its traditional social doctrines had no specific to offer, and were merely repeated, when, in order to be effective, they should have been thought out again from the beginning and formulated in new and living terms." The traditional teaching "had insisted that all men were brethren. But it did not occur to it to point out that, as a result of the new economic imperialism which was beginning to develop in the seventeenth century, the brethren of the English merchant were the Africans whom he kidnapped for slavery in America, or the American Indians whom he stripped of their lands, or the Indian craftsmen from whom he bought muslins and silks at starvation prices." The new economic society abandoned "the social doctrines advanced from the pulpit," as "their practical ineffectiveness prepared the way for their theoretical abandonment. . . . The social teaching of the Church had ceased to count, because the Church itself had ceased to think."[3]

Some people may have the sense that referring to those old Bible texts doesn't make much sense anymore, as the era of the traditional economy has long past. To such objections we reply that these texts always point to the faith aspect; that's why, although they do not give economic prescriptions, they do give an understanding of the economic perspective, even for our modern times. Our economy too must concern itself with justice. But, as Tawney observes, we have to think through the Bible texts from the bottom up and reformulate them in new and viable terms. To do that is impossible without knowledge of economic matters and without employing "all your mind" (Matt. 22:37). Yet the cardinal question to be asked is simple: to whom or what does the economic science pay allegiance and to which sort of laws are current practices subject? A small book like this one on "the Bible and economics" cannot provide that insight by itself.

3. Richard H. Tawney, *Religion and the Rise of Capitalism: A Historical Study* (New York: Harcourt, Brace, 1926).

Still others find the Bible relevant, but draw different conclusions. They point to the fact that biblical economic thinking is pre-capitalistic and consider that to be the ideal world. This often goes hand in hand with the romanticizing of "community," focusing on the family and the family household, on the small agrarian or village community. As if these traditional communities always were so open-minded! "Today the word 'community' is a different term for 'lost paradise,'" maintains Zygmunt Bauman.[4] However, a community can be terribly cruel and display the utmost forms of oppression and exclusion. "Back to the community" or "let's form a commune" cannot be the slogan. Indeed, toward the end of the Middle Ages people said, "The air of the city makes you free!"

The fact is that often under the guise of appealing to "traditional values," fascist propaganda is enacted. In Argentina under military dictatorship, the battle cry was, "God, fatherland, family, private property." The potential blessings of modern society had to be eliminated. Jesus himself criticized the absolutization of the family (Matt. 10:37). We may not turn family into an idol; nor communities, for that matter, which sometimes have to be severed or even broken up. The American sociologist Richard Sennett points to the example of the inward-turning group cohesion of the American white labor class, which manifested itself in the refusal to identify itself with those who were engaged in non-union occupations, with the liberal elite (and the resulting counter-cultural tendency in their children), and with poor blacks, the latter of whom they often regarded as parasites who fraudulently obtained welfare.[5]

We must not judge traditional communities according to today's criteria. However, when we view them from an economic-anthropological angle, they are useful to teach us about our individualized society. They no doubt teach us, in their internal relationships, about the real purpose of the economy. Economics literally means the arrangement of the "home," the place where we all live. Globalization has served to make it possible to observe everybody at their home-base. Generally speaking, in every economic order there are three kinds of mechanisms at work simultaneously. The economic act of the one individual is not only in tune with the next

4. Zygmunt Bauman, *Community: Seeking Safety in an Insecure World* (Cambridge: Cambridge University Press, 2001).

5. Richard Sennett, *Respect: The Formation of Character in an Age of Inequality* (New York: Norton, 2003).

person but also fits in with the overall picture. Thus we find (1) reciprocity, which is the customary system of mutual donations; (2) redistribution; and (3) exchange. Societal life as a whole presupposes reciprocal acts of expression. In spite of the disparity in traditional societies, their inhabitants could feel that they occupied a respectable place. Its communality found its expression in rituals of inequality. The modern market economy, however, has elevated commercial exchange to dominant status. But the segregation and the duality it causes are uneconomical, as we discussed in Chapter 16.

Christian social thinking, social democracy, and even classical democratic liberalism have all understood that the three above-mentioned economic principles must also be carried over into the field of the modern market economy, not only to correct it — through subsidies, income and taxation policies — but also to help it in a healthy way through investments in the infrastructure and through anti-trust policies. The Dutch lawyer and former minister of justice J. H. Donner has remarked, "Self interest and individual action by themselves do not create community bonds and a sound government. Thinking in these terms is based on a view of humanity that does not offer a counterweight against the centrifugal powers it creates. Naturally, I can analyze and find a reason with my brains; I can relativize, but I cannot give structure and evaluate; that requires a point of view from outside."

The economy in biblical times had no inkling of the macro-problems of the current world economy. Yet economic actions took place according to the same principles of donation, redistribution, and exchange, the same as today. However in those days economic life took place predominantly within the confines of the family household. It's no surprise that the author of Proverbs, when he wants to praise the virtue of good housekeeping, singles out the woman, the real manager of the home economy. From Africa to the poor districts in the large American cities we observe how it is women who, often alone, are busy in the home to engage in meeting needs, which, according to the textbooks, is the central function of the economy. In Lima, Peru, tens of thousands of women together look after the communal kitchens to feed their families and neighbors. In millions of agrarian family households, in villages, farms, and ethnic communities it is the "community" that organizes the economy and is the basis for economic development. The disruption of this community-based economy which we call "development" is an immense structural mistake. The community itself must decide how to participate in the market economy based on its own strengths and on its own terms.

J. H. Boeke, in his book about the Indonesian economy, describes how he, in the 1930s, when Indonesia still was a Dutch colony, observed the difference in economic actions between women and men in a village market place on Java. The women roamed everywhere, while the men gathered in small groups. The women were engaged in looking for and shopping for the daily needs. The men were not interested in this sort of trade at all; they were engaged in accumulation, not distribution. The women paid with the local currency, mostly small change; the men used the currency issued by the colonial power. The trading done by the women centered on consumers' needs, while the men acted as commercial producers. He observed that the women bought a great variety of articles, while the men specialized in the trade of one or two cash crops. The women showed up on a daily basis while the men's presence was determined by the seasons. The women moved freely in the open market space, while the men stuck close to the official agent employed by the colonial authorities. The women bought at fixed, traditional, thus reliable prices, while the men's actions were subjected to an unstable fluctuating price structure. The women paid cash; the men engaged in risky credit arrangements.[6]

From an economic and sociological perspective women generally are interested in use value, not primarily in the commodity value of goods. In a "use value" economy, money serves to facilitate the exchange of goods into other goods; in the "commodity value" economy, like the colonial one, it is the money that counts: it is invested to acquire more money, which causes the economic goods to have only an instrumental, secondary function.

No market economy can function without use values. No paid labor can occur without "shadow labor," those essential functions at home and in the entire community, activities, in essence, which keep the market afloat. However, it is the acquisition principle of the commercial economy that exercises the greatest power. It has a large-scale, even worldwide organization and is served by the most advanced technology.

Researchers on the colonial economy prior to World War II sharply distinguished between East and West. In both economies today production is

6. J. H. Boeke, *Economics and Economic Policy of Dual Societies, as Exemplified by Indonesia* (Haarlem: H. D. Tjeenk Willink, 1953).

highly organized — including and even especially in what the modern economist (rather contemptuously) labels the "unorganized" traditional sector — but the West has neglected the organization of consumption, the satisfying of needs, which is supposed to be the goal of the economy. "It's here where the danger lies for the Western civilization. It's to this that the people of the countries who are the unwilling recipients of the Western advantages fundamentally object. The test of a civilized society is not the increased growth of new needs, but of new activities, and these are not promoted by the organized production."[7]

The capable woman in Proverbs 31 is also, according to our understanding, an "all-round" person in her economic actions, just as are innumerable women in Africa and elsewhere in the world. "She perceives that her merchandise is profitable." "She is like the ships of the merchant, she brings her food from far away." "She works with willing hands." She knows how to invest prudently: "with the fruit of her hands she plants a vineyard." And then it is naturally added: she sees the needs of all people within her neighborhood. She acts "without favoritism" (James 2:1). As a real economist, "she opens her hands to the poor and reaches out her hands to the needy."

The Italian nun Frances Cabrini, who near the end of the nineteenth century was engaged in social work in the poor workers' section of Chicago, was quite conservative in her beliefs. Her educational foundation rested on discipline and order. Yet she was deeply loved by the people. Richard Sennett has an explanation for this, which he calls both a theological statement as well as a personal opinion: "the religious notion of sin affects all persons with impartiality and carries no stigma."[8]

7. J. S. Furnivall, "The Organization of Consumption," *The Economic Journal*, March 1910.

8. Sennett, *Respect*.

CHAPTER 21

Globalization from the Bottom Up

You shall not covet your neighbor's house; you shall not covet your neighbor's wife, or male or female slave, or ox, or donkey, or anything that belongs to your neighbor.

EXODUS 20:17

For Jews demand signs and Greeks desire wisdom, but we proclaim Christ crucified, a stumbling block to Jews, and foolishness to Gentiles, but to those who are the called, both Jews and Greeks, Christ the power of God and the wisdom of God. For God's foolishness is wiser than human wisdom, and God's weakness is stronger than human strength.

1 CORINTHIANS 1:22-25

Build houses and live in them; plant gardens and eat what they produce. Take wives and have sons and daughters; take wives for your sons, and give your daughters in marriage, that they may bear sons and daughters; multiply there and do not decrease. But seek the welfare of the city where I have sent you into exile, and pray to the LORD on its behalf, for in its welfare you will find your welfare.

JEREMIAH 29:5-7

E conomic development has disturbed the tranquility of villages in Asia and elsewhere in the world. Indeed, we could even say that by and large the entire traditional economy of the Third World has, in many cases, been ruined beyond repair. Millions of people live on the edge. Jacques Ellul speaks eloquently to this:

> Collective greatness comes only at the price of individual blood-shed and unhappiness. There is no other way. The splendid ideology of harmonious growth in which the general interest would be simply the sum-total of the prosperities of individuals, and would converge to produce collective development, is nothing but an idyll. We can predict with certainty that all the peoples whose states are now committed to development are unhappy peoples, and that their unhappiness will intensify as development becomes more rapid. Sadly enough, the West has already shown the way in this respect, for the West had already made the proletarian class more wretched than it had been before, and it was on the incredible suffering of this class that the grand and glorious "technological society" was built. The glory was so great that the countries can now think of nothing but imitating the West; they forget the price that was paid, and lull themselves with the dream that this kind of power can be acquired without paying for it.[1]

When we speak of "the war on poverty," we should realize that modern poverty is a product of history, that it has, to a large degree, been caused by the destructive expansion of Western interests. Bartolomé de las Casas saw the initial disastrous developments of this process before his own eyes (see Chapter 19). However, the scales fell off his eyes when he worked on his Pentecost sermon in 1514 and he saw that our development aid is, in a certain sense, unjustly acquired property (Sirach 34:21).

We cannot blame lack of witnessing on the part of prophets and martyrs. Neither can we get away with abandoning the world, as many religious idealists would do. On the contrary: we have to be engaged in the building of a just economy. In Chapter 8 we saw that the core of the Ten

---

1. Jacques Ellul, *The Betrayal of the West*, trans. Matthew J. O'Connell (New York: Seabury, 1978).

Commandments is to help those who need help. This "housekeeping" prescription, which deals with the arranging of our economy, the household we share with all people, is not a prohibition like the other commandments, but an invitation to act creatively.

The debate by earlier Christians directed against interest and profit belongs to the past. Times have changed: we live now in a "society of risk." The prayer in Psalm 119:36, "Turn my heart to your testimonies, and not to gain" is at complete odds with our dominating economic culture. However, we cannot do away with profit and the market. The woman in the last chapter of Proverbs is a highly capable businesswoman, as we saw in the previous chapter. When James in his letter criticizes people who assert that "today or tomorrow we'll go to such and such a town and spend a year there, doing business and making money," he doesn't condemn the making of profit, but he condemns the casual way in which this statement is made. To boast this way is wrong (James 4:16), "for you are a mist that appears for a little while and then vanishes." What we have to say and live is, "If the Lord wishes, we will live and do this or that" (James 4:15). Riches are not in themselves the source of evil — they are seen in the Bible also as a source of blessings — but rather the exploitation that can be the source of that wealth is evil. It is the rich person who receives a warning not to regard his wealth as a source of pride.

We cannot deal with poverty and oppression in a tautological way; in other words, we cannot address poverty by using the instruments which were the cause of the problems in the first place. Poverty does not originate out of nowhere, and cannot be fought in isolation, the way we deal with the symptoms of an illness. We first have to fathom the ideology of this technological era. Our point of departure starts elsewhere.

John Locke, one of the founding fathers of liberalism, the philosophy that has developed the idea of scarcity, was clearly aware that scarcity had nothing to do with the availability of sufficient goods. Even though Locke had to admit that in his world there was more than enough for everybody, even if the world population doubled, the modern economy became established on the idea of scarcity thanks to the invention of money. Economic theory has defined the economic problem in such a way that it, in principle, cannot be solved, because economic needs are regarded as infinite. Locke wrote, "invent something that can be used as money . . . and the result will be that this same person who initially was sufficiently satisfied with what he had for himself and his family, suddenly starts to increase his possessions."[2] Regardless of the ideology of "equality," it's this craving for more that infects people, and causes them sooner or later to clash with their equals. Ultimately it results in the arising of what René Girard calls the "mimetic" or imitative desire, that is, the desire to copy behavior. People begin to want what others have and to want to be like others.[3] And so the tenth commandment, "You shall not covet anything that is your neighbor's," becomes diametrically opposed to our culture. In the society of equality, desire becomes king.

We have seen that the standard for "progress" is "progress" itself; that the social and cultural havoc caused by the Technique, is being fought with technical means (see Chapter 15). Yet this is no different from evicting the devil with the help of Beelzebub, the chief of devils. If we want to prevent assimilation into our technical-economical world, we must use non-technical means. We must proceed with a vision that is independent of technical success. Only when we are equipped with a worldview that is not influenced by the technical system can we confront the Technique in order to mold it so that it can fit into a non-technicist framework that is compatible with our humanity. Only then will money no longer be the dominating force, but rather an instrument through which an amicable economy can be established (see Chapter 11). But money is not the only factor. In fact, it's not even the most successful. Countless development projects have been killed by financing and countless local pricing systems have been derailed through the shock effects of the invasions of Western capital.

It would be wrong to relate the identity of the poor to their being economically oppressed. The poor person is more than an oppressed person. The poor are not just victims, conveniently displayed on pictures to be used in money-raising campaigns. Even our analysis of the poverty problem, however overwhelming it is, may not remain confined to the aspect of oppression. A human being goes beyond that: "Before I was humbled" — before I was oppressed, before I suffered — "I went astray" (Ps. 119:67). We all have an existence apart from oppression. That has nothing to do with submission or passiveness. "I have done what is just and right; do not leave me to my oppressors" (Ps. 119:121). But the poor are not always correct. "You shall not be partial to the poor in a lawsuit" (Exod. 23:3).

2. John Locke, *Two Treatises of Government* (London: Everyman's Library, 1982).

3. René Girard, *The Scapegoat*, trans. Yvonne Freccero (Baltimore: Johns Hopkins University Press, 1986).

Exodus states something else as well: "You shall not follow the majority in wrongdoing; when you bear witness in a lawsuit, you shall not side with the majority so as to pervert justice" (Exod. 23:2). This text is one of the most important eye-openers in the entire Bible. The majority. Everything and everybody. But I — nevertheless! — I know different (see Chapter 15). Here we encounter René Girard's surprising biblical insight. The Bible is a unique religious body of writings, completely different from and totally opposite to mythological and religious texts in history. Girard does not read the Bible as a theologian, but he looks at it from the point of view of a cultural scientist, and discovers that it is a book that distinguishes itself from the entire canon of world literature.

"To follow the majority in wrongdoing": those who follow the crowd and the usurpers who manipulate it also claim to do God's work. But those are the gods who are in tune with the crowd; they are the ones who cause the downfall of the dissenters, those who dare to be different, the just, of which Job was one. They drag in God to lend credibility to their persecution of those who are nonconforming, who have a divergent opinion. Job's friends are the demagogues who have set the tone, because they have God in their pocket. Job is the culprit. He is pushed aside "without further investigation" (Job 34:24), without them analyzing what's really going on. The envy and the revenge of the multitude coincide with what they see as God's revenge.[4]

Girard points out that the peace and order in a social organization, which give it cohesion and form its culture, are achieved by manipulating public opinion, which requires the killing of a scapegoat in the form of a dissenting person or group of persons which have been persecuted by manipulated public opinion.[5] Jesus' death on the cross is, in the history of culture and religion, a unique happening. "Jews demand signs and the Greeks desire wisdom, but we proclaim Christ crucified" (1 Cor. 1:22-23). The term "Jews and Greeks" in Paul's world is essentially saying "all peoples." It's not unique that Jesus is the scapegoat; neither that he was innocent; he is among the many innocent victims in history who perished through organized persecution. The medieval witch-hunts come to mind, instigated to restore peace and order in society. Of course Jesus is the preeminent personification of innocence, not called a goat, but rather the "Lamb of God." He has been unjustly convicted and the collective hate against him is un-

---

4. René Girard, *I See Satan Fall Like Lightning* (New York: Orbis Books, 2001).
5. Girard, *The Scapegoat.*

founded. But what is new about Jesus is that his innocence is explicitly proclaimed (Acts 3:14). This testimony continues until this day as the unmasking of and the victory over evil.

This is so new that in Western culture awareness has been created for the innocent as victim. The Bible reveals the truth regarding the scapegoat mechanism. It is not something that arose in the human heart, nor has it come out of mythology. That's why theologians may not idolize this suffering by regarding it more or less a metaphysical or mystical metaphor. When they do so they unknowingly play the same game as their opponents and as the entire mythology. Then they again are forced to elevate to sacred something that in the Gospels has been unmasked as violence.

To go to bat for victims is similar in all cultures, including in our individualistic society, but it usually is confined to members of the same group. In modern society we are acquainted with few people in such a direct personal relationship. But how about those anonymous people, either far away or close by, whom we see on television when calamities strike? Girard views our concern for victims beyond our own circle or family to be the unique cultural influence of the testimony about Jesus' innocent death and resurrection.

The concern for the innocent victim as such, regardless where they belong, is according to Girard the truly essential cause of globalization, of which the economic aspect may be the most noticeable but not the most significant. This is really quite surprising. And, indeed, when our media report what is happening to victims far away, they do this because they are victims. "The ascent of the victim as victim runs parallel with the arrival of the first genuine planetary culture." This worldwide phenomenon is the fruit of the care for the victim and not the other way around. The reaction in the aftermath of the tsunami that hit Asia and Africa on December 26, 2004, is a telling example of the emotions that resulted from a solidarity that was the result of globalization. Everywhere in the Western world financial assistance was so overwhelming that no further solicitation was needed. All this was done to help people we don't know, but who suffered and for whom society had formed the proper channels of response, and so created a public domain. The "public interest" went far beyond the level that could be provided by the modern economic system. It became and still becomes *bonum commune,* the common good, a public affair.

Jacques Ellul has remarked in his book *The Betrayal of the West* that the bad conscience of the West can be traced not to Greek or Roman thinking, but to our Christian heritage. It's the West that sees through the great damage caused by its own violence and exploitation. It's also in the West, notwithstanding the betrayal of its historical origins, where the matter of human rights has been broached and placed on the agenda.

The "war on poverty" is technicist terminology, suggesting that it is something like "the war on absenteeism," or "the fight against insects." This sort of wording places the poor person in the role of object, of some "technical element," of victim. Indeed, poverty has its millions of victims, but our "war" must take the form of a communal effort to create public space, a real commonwealth. Finally, the poor person needs to be respected in his or her own vision, as "economic subject."

Imagine a little city with few people in it. One day a great danger comes to this city. In the city lives a poor man with clear vision, but nobody notices him because they are all busy with their own pursuits. The shabby old man sees the world in such perspective that he could have rescued the city from its misery, but no one thinks to ask him because he is poor. He lacks the expertise; he has never consulted any of the "experts." We recognize this situation, of course, as a metaphor for our own. Yet we too have listened to the "shouting of a ruler among fools" and have surrendered ourselves to the manipulations of the media, nearly all of which tell us the same things, rather than "heeding the quiet words of the wise" (Eccles. 9:14-17).

Individualistic economic thinking deals with a very limited and materialistic understanding of work. Work means tilling the land, digging into the soil and mining for metals, controlling nature (Job 28:1-11). But, as the technician and theologian Dippel has remarked, "To increase production may be laudable, but it carries no ultimate solution." Robinson Crusoe usually serves as a model here, in view of his lonesome stay as a producer and consumer on an island. Dippel, however, stresses the fact that "to be busy in developing human relations, that is work too." We are responsible for the development of society. That is structural development. When we regard work as solely a matter of material production then, for instance, we solve international conflicts by means of war: through the production of weapons and the inevitable use of those weapons. The American war in Iraq is a good example of violent use of materials at enormous material expense. Dippel argues that it is a way "to avoid meeting the neighbor-enemy and a refusal to face him eye to eye." It is in the first place destructive and creates problems rather than solutions.[6]

Dippel calls the work that Robinson Crusoe was doing "primary." It points to those who are busy advancing their career, and also to the "employees," those who are "used" in the process; it embraces both managers and powerless. It also applies to the "few who squander their lives in a functional, specialized kind of job, totally taken in by their own specialty, while discovering too late that the clock, that first beneficial machine, really indicates a definite end of their life. They have experienced nobody and nothing but their own little part."[7] This, of course, echoes James 4:13-16.

But there are other kinds of labor. They only begin when the factory gates close. Dippel says the shutting of these gates is a lie, as if now work would stop. There are, however, three sorts of labor.

> Besides the work of the first kind, efforts which are the results of severing our direct relationship with nature, which is the productive, material labor, there is the work that is the result of the breakdown of our direct relationship with our fellow creatures. That's the labor of the second sort. Then there also is a virtual sea of labor that proceeds from the knowledge that the human race lives without a singular, visible, direct relationship with God and Eternity, labor of the third kind. We don't know in a direct way where we come from, nor where we are going, either before or after this short life in this cold and immense universe. We have to be told.[8]

And culture — of which we are all a part — consists of labor of the secondary and tertiary kind. It is labor which does not necessarily pollute nature. We must become actively engaged in matters of the economy, in this threefold sense. "Build houses and live therein. Plant gardens and eat what they produce" (Jer. 29:5). This is the prophet's message to the Jews who knew that their exile in Babylon would only be temporary. "Seek the welfare of the city and pray to the LORD on its behalf" (v. 7). Society building is work that encompasses work of the first kind — constructing

---

6. C. J. Dippel, *Verkenning en verwachting. Cultuurkritische opstellen* (The Hague: Boekencentrum, 1962)

7. Dippel, *Verkenning en verwachting.*

8. Dippel, *Verkenning en verwachting.*

houses, for example — but also of the second kind — seeking its welfare, its peace — and of the third kind as well — praying for it. Only then do we not function as agents, as the "employees" of the technicist system, and can we cope with the world without conducting ourselves in accordance with this world. Only then do we show ourselves as different, as people with a new vision. Only then are we in a position to discern the will of God and do "what is good and acceptable and perfect" (Rom. 12:2).

After all, we are aliens and transients (1 Chron. 29:15). The well-known twentieth-century American commentator Walter Lippmann has said, "Every one of us is, from a spiritual point of view, an immigrant." This means that we just don't step into the market without a critical view. If we do, we run the risk of conforming too readily to the world. We are also beyond the imperative on the rush to alter the structures. We do have to build them: that is labor of the second sort. Thorough investigation is necessary, which is not present where injustice abounds.

We must always be ready to "think globally and act locally." The rulers, the authorities, the cosmic powers (Eph. 6:12; the King James Bible speaks of the "principalities and powers" and the "rulers of darkness") are everywhere. The level of insight has to be deep enough to withstand the all-encompassing technicist culture with its totalitarian presumptions. That means that the labor of the second sort cannot be delegated to the automatic functions of the market. This would entail avoidance of responsibility. All this is hard work, but also joyful work, as reflected in Mark 12:30 — to be done not only with heart and soul, but also "with all your mind and with all your strength." The World Alliance of Reformed Churches (WARC) meeting in the coastal capital of Ghana, Accra, in August of 2004, issued the following declaration:

> We have heard that creation continues to groan, in bondage, waiting for its liberation (Rom. 8:22). We are challenged by the cries of the people who suffer and by the woundedness of creation itself. We see a dramatic convergence between the suffering of the people and the damage done to the rest of creation.
>
> We recognize the enormity and complexity of the situation. We do not seek simple answers. As seekers of truth and justice and looking through the eyes of powerless and suffering people, we see that the current world (dis)order is rooted in an extremely complex and immoral economic system defended by empire. In using the term

"empire" we mean the coming together of economic, cultural, political and military power that constitutes a system of domination led by powerful nations to protect and defend their own interests.[9]

Over against this *force majeure,* this superior power, the churches' rebuttal is that in the choices we make on behalf of economic justice, the integrity of our faith in God is at stake. This means that we don't look at the system from within, but from elsewhere: with the eyes of powerless and suffering humanity. In the economy this means that there is a big job to do. Many want to look at it from a political angle, or desire a readymade (technical!) solution. Many commentators, either out of ignorance or cynicism, ridiculed the WARC document, labeling it an example of outdated, decades-old theology.

This declaration, however, has the character of a confession. It is not full of old-fashioned theological jargon and it also lacks the illusions that often accompany such writing. The document doesn't pretend to change the world by spouting stereotypical political statements. On the contrary, it points to the radical consequences of this world order.

The entire statement has been composed constantly referring to the Bible — something that was also characteristic of revolutionary thinking among Christians in the 1960s, but certainly no reason to label the document outdated. The WARC wants to call us to give account of the economic reality in the world. The immense dramas in Sudan, Iraq, Congo, Africa south of the Sahara — the summation is endless, and these disasters cannot be seen as outside the global context — cannot be described in small print. That's why, through biblical references, words can be found that point to the severe famine conditions and the real persecution there. The declaration recognizes "the enormity and complexity of the situation." The totalitarian character of the technical system which lies at the bottom of these problems, and which threatens every alternative communal initiative with disappearance or assimilation, cannot be countered without a basically changed attitude over against the system itself. Only when there is a profound measure of contemplation, as was done in Accra, can matters change.

From that spiritual level emerges a perspective for implementation. We must enter the arena with a "bridging device," as Ellul would say: we have to provide a link that goes back to the original process and from there

---

9. World Alliance of Reformed Churches, "The Accra Declaration: Covenanting for Justice in the Economy and the Earth," 2004. Available online at http://www.oikos.nl.

infuse the matter with new information. Instead of extinguishing a fire here and there by means of a "development project," the real solution is of a structural-economic nature: we have to start by the source of the technicist process in order to change the entirety of its course and organization, by the introduction of new information sources. The current market practices must be rethought from their very inception. Only those who engage in "three kinds of labor" can impart to the technique the external, nontechnical truth. In the global trade the goal is to free all links in the chain from impurities and then weld them together. The business community and those who practice fair trade call this "chain responsibility," a consequence of corporate social responsibility.

This requires a close coordination of effort between South and North. It means that the market is not assumed to be a given. Exploitation and exclusion must be replaced by the development of new, honest, lasting, and environmentally friendly markets. This would benefit not only some remote places of the world, but would also be inviting and appealing to the mainstream of existing enterprises, who would want to come on board out of societally responsible considerations. Here, as well as in so many other places in the global household, is it possible for the "salt of the earth" carried in by the laborers of a just economy to be nothing else but saltiness (Matt. 5:13).

The "far neighbor" is far away, indeed, yet he or she is without a doubt part of our economic network. We do have an economic relationship with the plantation laborer and the small coffee or banana farmer far away, as we influence their economic well-being. After all, we buy their coffee, their bananas, their clothes. The modern economy has made the small producer all but invisible, but via the transparency of fair trade we obtain a clear vision of the life of the cotton farmer and the woman at the sewing machine. In that way we cancel out their anonymity and their arbitrary exchangeability and, to some extent, make true the biblical command to share our bread with the hungry, by helping the neighbor in acquiring his primary sustenance — not in the way of one-sided aid, but through cooperative labor of the second kind, fostering an honest and transparent organization of production, commerce, and consumption.

Rich people cannot do the developing for the poor, who must do that themselves, but they must respect them in that goal and give them room to do so. Globalization must be a joint effort from the bottom up.

Our task is to "rebuild the ancient ruins" in the damaged world-city (Isa. 58:12). "In its welfare you will find your welfare."

Economic Comments
by John Maynard Keynes

. . . for the first time since his creation man will be faced with his real, his permanent problem — how to use his freedom from pressing economic cares, how to occupy the leisure, which science and compound interest will have won for him, to live wisely and agreeably and well.

The strenuous purposeful money-makers may carry all of us along with them into the lap of economic abundance. But it will be those peoples, who can keep alive, and cultivate into a fuller perfection, the art of life itself and do not sell themselves for the means of life, who will be able to enjoy the abundance when it comes.

Yet there is no country and no people, I think, who can look forward to the age of leisure and abundance without a dread. For we have been trained too long to strive and not to enjoy. It is a fearful problem for the ordinary person, with no special talents, to occupy himself, especially if he no longer has roots in the soil or in custom or in the beloved conventions of a traditional society. To judge from the behavior and the achievements of the wealthy classes today in any quarter of the world, the outlook is very depressing! For these are, so to speak, our advance guard — those who are spying out the promised land for the rest of us and pitching their camp there. For they have most of them failed disastrously, so it seems to me —

Excerpt from John Maynard Keynes, "Economic Possibilities for Our Grandchildren," in *Essays in Persuasion* (New York: W.W. Norton & Company, 1963), pp. 358-73. This essay originally appeared in *The Nation and Atheneum,* October 11 and 18, 1930.

those who have an independent income but no associations or duties or ties — to solve the problem which has been set them.

I see us free to return to some of the most sure and certain principles of religion and traditional virtue — that avarice is a vice, that the exaction of usury is a misdemeanor, and the love of money is detestable, that those walk most truly in the paths of virtue and sane wisdom who take least thought for the morrow. We shall once more value ends above means and prefer the good to the useful. We shall honor those who can teach us how to pluck the hour and the day virtuously and well, the delightful people who are capable of taking direct enjoyment in things, the lilies of the field who toil not, neither do they spin.

Index of Scripture References